A Woman's
Book 2
Inner Life

Unlimited! ... Bible Studies for Today's Pentecostal Woman

*Arlene Allen, Peggy Musgrove,
Lori O'Dea, & Candy Tolbert*

GPH
Gospel Publishing House
Springfield, Missouri
02-0276

CONTENTS

FOREWORD

The multi-tasking world of the twenty-first century woman is unique. This era places demands on women previous eras never did. The necessity of having roots deep in God's Word and in His presence is as critical as at any other time in history. The woman of God who seeks His wisdom from consistent study of the Bible will find her life rooted through even the most volatile of life's challenges.

Stability comes when followers of Jesus take seriously the necessary and regular task of thorough study and meditation on God's Word. The "rootedness" so necessary for steady growth with the Lord is the intentional focus of this book, *A Woman's Inner Life.*

Your collaborators in this significant journey to strengthen your inner life bring years of spiritual maturity to this task. These four authors, Arlene Allen, Peggy Musgrove, Lori O'Dea, and Candy Tolbert, work together to make sure each lesson is not only biblically sound, but also connects you to women in the Bible who have faced similar challenges and whose lives can inspire you to serve the Lord in the good times and the daily challenges you face.

Because this study is written in an intentional manner, you will benefit most if you utilize each of the four authors' segments for each lesson. View them as doorways to the life-changing work of the Spirit. Each offers a different angle with which to view the topic. The introduction in one lesson may be your connecting point. In the next lesson, it may be the Bible study or the application of that study. The doorway that may connect all concepts of the lesson may be in the focus on a woman in the Bible who personifies the theme.

This study focuses on the central task of building up your inner life. The John 15 image of vine and branches is a picture of the struggle in our everyday lives. Nineteenth century Quaker writer Hannah Whitehall Smith wrote, "God's plan for us therefore is to get possession of the inside of a man, to take control and management of his will, and to work it for him; and then obedience is easy and a delight, and service becomes perfect freedom."[1]

A Woman's Inner Life is an effort to focus on "God's plan" as Hannah Whitehall Smith called it. Your study focuses on foundational truths that unfortunately get left out of the lives of too many followers of Christ. Foundational does not mean remedial; but reflects substantive themes from the Bible that are the spiritual DNA of the disciplined Christian life. Reflecting on your salvation, your participation with God's people, the building blocks of intimacy with the Lord, and the role of the Holy Spirit in your life will allow you to participate in "a long obedience in the same direction."[2]

The authors of this study believe that the building up of a woman's inner life is superintended by the Holy Spirit. Hunger for God is met by the Holy Spirit's constant focus on Jesus Christ. An early Pentecostal missionary and writer described this process personally when she said, "When the Spirit came in fullness as on the Day of Pentecost, it seemed to me as if He took me by the hand and led me into the very heart of God the Father, to show me how He was rejoicing over Jesus, the Son of His love. . . . It was from the point of view of the heart of God, where the Holy Spirit told me I had now come to abide."[3]

I commend to you the best efforts of four women whose sole desire is to help you abide in the depths of the life of Christ. Your "inner life" will be strengthened and you will become a reflection of what Psalm 1 pictures as a deeply rooted tree that produces fruit regardless of the circumstances.

Byron D. Klaus

President

Assemblies of God Theological Seminary

---

[1]Hannah Whitehall Smith, *The Christian's Secret of a Happy Life* (chapter 10), http://www.ccel.org/s/smith_hw/secret/secret13.htm (accessed 9/10/2004).

[2]Eugene H. Peterson, *A Long Obedience in the Same Direction,* (Downers Grove, Ill.: InterVarsity Press, 2000).

[3]Everett Wilson and Ruth Wilson, "Alice Luce: A Visionary Victorian" in *Portraits of a Generation,* ed. James R. Goff and Grant Wacker, (Fayetteville, Ark.: University of Arkansas Press, 2002) 163.

PREFACE

This series of Bible studies was written in response to women and pastors across the United States asking for Pentecostal studies to use in their churches for a group study or as individual study material.

A Woman's Inner Life is a Pentecostal study written by Pentecostal women. This study will be unique to any you have used before because the Pentecostal perspective is written into each lesson. The student will not have to search for the Pentecostal viewpoint—she needs only to embrace it and ask Jesus to help her apply it.

All who welcome Jesus Christ as Lord of their lives are reborn spiritually, receiving new life from God. Through faith in Christ, this new birth changes us from the inside out—rearranging our attitudes, desires, and motives.

What we are going to become is developed in the hours we spend with God, allowing Him to remake us. Both quantity and quality are to be considered here. A few minutes "caught on the run" is not sufficient for God to develop His character in us.

Soup carried in a tureen high over a waiter's head is unseen. No one knows what's inside the tureen—unless the waiter is bumped and stumbles. In the same way, people don't know what's inside us until we're bumped. If Christ is living in us and changing us from the inside out, what spills out is the fruit of the Spirit.

May these studies be a guide to help you examine your inner life. Ask God to help you grow as you apply what you will learn.

Arlene Allen
Director, Women's Ministries Department
General Council of the Assemblies of God

Her Vibrant Faith

CATCHING SIGHT
Introduction

*T*HE FOREMAN'S SIGNAL releases the giant ball. With dynamite force and a reverberating crash it meets the wall, crumbling bricks and scattering fragments of mortar. Repeatedly, the powerful pendulum swings reducing the barrier to rubble to be carted away so construction can begin.

Life has many walls and fences that divide, separate, and compartmentalize. Not made of wood or stone, these barriers are personal obstructions, blocking people from each other and from God. But Christ came to tear down the sin partition separating us from God and blast the barriers keeping us from each other. His death and Resurrection opened the way to receive eternal life, to bring all who believe into a relationship with Him, and to facilitate believers' relationships with one another.

Some think of Christianity in terms of what it forbids. When they consider what it means to be a Christian, they think of what they are separated from instead of what they are separated to.

Each person has been given an invitation to have a personal relationship with Jesus. It is not enough to hear wonderful stories about His life. You need to become part of the story yourself.

GETTING FOCUSED

Begin your study by considering the following:

What separates you from developing a close relationship with Christ? If you have accepted Christ, but haven't allowed Him to totally change your life, are you really saved?

BIBLE READING

John 3:1–21

New International Version

1 Now there was a man of the Pharisees named Nicodemus, a member of the Jewish ruling council. 2 He came to Jesus at night and said, "Rabbi, we know you are a teacher who has come from God. For no one could perform the miraculous signs you are doing if God were not with him."

3 In reply Jesus declared, "I tell you the truth, no one can see the kingdom of God unless he is born again."

4 "How can a man be born when he is old?" Nicodemus asked. "Surely he cannot enter a second time into his mother's womb to be born!"

5 Jesus answered, "I tell you the truth, no one can enter the kingdom of God unless he is born of water and the Spirit. 6 Flesh gives birth to flesh, but the Spirit gives birth to spirit. 7 You should not be surprised at my saying, 'You must be born again.' 8 The wind blows wherever it pleases. You hear its sound, but you cannot tell where it

New Living Translation

1 After dark one evening, a Jewish religious leader named Nicodemus, a Pharisee, 2 came to speak with Jesus. "Teacher," he said, "we all know that God has sent you to teach us. Your miraculous signs are proof enough that God is with you."

3 Jesus replied, "I assure you, unless you are born again, you can never see the Kingdom of God."

4 "What do you mean?" exclaimed Nicodemus. "How can an old man go back into his mother's womb and be born again?"

5 Jesus replied, "The truth is, no one can enter the Kingdom of God without being born of water and the Spirit. 6 Humans can reproduce only human life, but the Holy Spirit gives new life from heaven. 7 So don't be surprised at my statement that you must be born again. 8 Just as you can hear the wind but can't tell where it comes from or where it is going, so you can't explain how people are born of the Spirit."

9 "What do you mean?"

New International Version

comes from or where it is going. So it is with everyone born of the Spirit."

9 "How can this be?" Nicodemus asked.

10 "You are Israel's teacher," said Jesus, "and do you not understand these things? 11 I tell you the truth, we speak of what we know, and we testify to what we have seen, but still you people do not accept our testimony. 12 I have spoken to you of earthly things and you do not believe; how then will you believe if I speak of heavenly things? 13 No one has ever gone into heaven except the one who came from heaven—the Son of Man. 14 Just as Moses lifted up the snake in the desert, so the Son of Man must be lifted up, 15 that everyone who believes in him may have eternal life.

16 "For God so loved the world that he gave his one and only Son, that whoever believes in him shall not perish but have eternal life. 17 For God did not send his Son into the world to condemn the world, but to save the world through him. 18 Whoever believes in him is not condemned, but whoever does not believe stands condemned already because he has not believed in the name of God's one and only Son. 19 This is the verdict: Light has come into the world, but men loved darkness instead of light

New Living Translation

Nicodemus asked.

10 Jesus replied, "You are a respected Jewish teacher, and yet you don't understand these things? 11 I assure you, I am telling you what we know and have seen, and yet you won't believe us. 12 But if you don't even believe me when I tell you about things that happen here on earth, how can you possibly believe if I tell you what is going on in heaven? 13 For only I, the Son of Man, have come to earth and will return to heaven again. 14 And as Moses lifted up the bronze snake on a pole in the wilderness, so I, the Son of Man, must be lifted up on a pole, 15 so that everyone who believes in me will have eternal life.

16 "For God so loved the world that he gave his only Son, so that everyone who believes in him will not perish but have eternal life. 17 God did not send his Son into the world to condemn it, but to save it. 18 There is no judgment awaiting those who trust him. But those who do not trust him have already been judged for not believing in the only Son of God. 19 Their judgment is based on this fact: The light from heaven came into the world, but they loved the darkness more than the light, for their actions were evil. 20 They hate the light because they want to sin in the darkness. They stay away from the light for fear their sins will be

New International Version	New Living Translation
because their deeds were evil. 20 Everyone who does evil hates the light, and will not come into the light for fear that his deeds will be exposed. 21 But whoever lives by the truth comes into the light, so that it may be seen plainly that what he has done has been done through God."	exposed and they will be punished. 21 But those who do what is right come to the light gladly, so everyone can see that they are doing what God wants."

GAINING BIBLICAL INSIGHT
Living in relationship with my Savior

Nicodemus could wait no longer. There was something about Jesus he had to know: What set this man apart from all other teachers? Only a prophet from God could do miracles as He did, yet He was so different from other teachers. Nicodemus so desperately wanted to know he willingly came to discuss religious issues. Jesus surprised him by turning the conversation to discuss a living faith.

Faith Born of the Spirit

Nicodemus spent his life pursuing religious issues. Trained in the law, he was a ruler of the Pharisees who meticulously kept both the Mosaic Law and the "traditions of the elders" in an effort to gain God's favor. Here was a Man who did not belong to their group, yet God's hand was evidently upon Him.

Exactly why Nicodemus came at night, we do not know. Was it for privacy? Fear of others? Time limitations? Whatever his reasons, he opened the discussion with a tentative statement.

Jesus went quickly to the heart of the issue. In essence He said, "Being part of the kingdom of God is not based on what you do, but who you are. To see the kingdom, you have to be born into it."

Nicodemus's reaction shows his natural point of view. He understood the importance of birth. His people kept lengthy genealogies

which gave them identity. Wasn't that what being born into the kingdom meant? Any other form of birth was impossible in his thinking,
but Jesus was talking about life in a different dimension.

Jesus said, "Flesh gives birth to flesh but the Spirit gives birth to
spirit" (verse 6). Spiritual birth is necessary to enter God's spiritual
kingdom. Neither physical birth nor a life of rule keeping can move a
person from the realm of flesh to the realm of the Spirit.

**If rule keeping does not earn a place in God's kingdom, why
should a person who has experienced spiritual birth seek to
honor God's laws?**

To help Nicodemus understand life in another dimension, Jesus
made a comparison to the wind which is unseen but undeniably exis-
tent. "So it is with everyone born of the Spirit (verse 8)," He said,
describing the invisible but real experience of becoming spiritually
alive by the Holy Spirit. This spiritual birth, sometimes called conver-
sion, is the basis of a vibrant, living faith. With this new birth comes
the desire to live in right relationship with God and a desire to please
Him by keeping His laws.

Faith Made Possible by the Cross of Christ

Incredulous, Nicodemus pursued the issue. Still caught up with
"doing," he asked about the logistics of spiritual birth. "If you cannot
enter the kingdom by keeping the laws of a holy God, how can it
happen?"

Nicodemus was well versed in the Old Testament. Had he thoroughly understood those writings, he would have known salvation
was not earned.

Zeroing in on Nicodemus's Old Testament knowledge, Jesus
reminded him of the people who were healed in obedience to God's
command to look at a bronze serpent hung on a pole in the desert
(Numbers 21:8,9). Jesus then made a subtle reference to His own

future death on the Cross by saying, "Just as Moses lifted up the snake in the desert, so the Son of Man must be lifted up, that everyone who believes in him may have eternal life" (verses 14,15).

This statement clearly outlines God's plan for our salvation. What is God's part of the plan? What is our part?

Jesus' sacrificial death broke the barrier that separates sinful man from a holy God. No man, however good his life, can ever cross that barrier by his own effort. Those who believe in Christ experience spiritual birth through His atoning work. Then they begin the incredible faith-walk in living relationship with Him.

Faith Rooted in the Love of God

Knowing Nicodemus's thoughts, Jesus continued teaching, telling of God's amazing love for mankind. This view of God was different than the view Nicodemus may have had. Those who meticulously kept laws usually viewed God as a Being of fierce judgment. Jesus dealt with this view by talking first about God's love which planned for man's salvation.

Read John 3:16 and spend some time meditating on God's love which initiated our salvation. **What difference does it make if you view God first as a God of love, then as a God of judgment?**

God's love initiated our salvation but that does not mean He is not a God of judgment. Jesus went on to explain that fact (verses 17 and 18). He did not come to condemn the world but to save people from the condemnation they were already under because of unbelief.

Jesus described those who do not believe, as living in darkness. Those who choose to live by faith He said are living in light. **What contrasts between these lifestyles do you see in this passage?**

Jesus paints a clear picture of two ways of life. We can live in darkness away from God's light, which would expose our evil deeds, or we can live in God's light and truth so all can plainly see what God can do through us. The choice is ours. When we make the choice of living in light and truth, we enter into a living relationship with God that is eternal, affecting not only this life but the life to come.

Mary Magdalene was one woman who made the choice to leave a life of darkness. Her encounter with Jesus changed her life forever. When by faith she received deliverance from her past, she followed Jesus all the way to the Cross and was one of the first to know of His Resurrection.

REFLECTING HIS IMAGE
Mary Magdalene (Matthew 28:5,6; John 19:25; 20:1–18)

More than grief and bewilderment brought me to that gloomy place of mourning. For me, watching Jesus die a horrible death was like losing my entire family in one afternoon. His life gave me hope. His words gave me life. Suddenly He was dead. And so I stayed at the tomb.

My adolescence was nothing like yours, unless you had a nickname like "mad Mary" and spent years with hair matted and disheveled, and sore-infested, bloody skin from self-inflicted cuts. Depression drove me to fits of rage. A force beyond my control plagued me with a compulsive desire to curse God by name. In short, I was rendered insane by the power of evil spirits. Seven to be exact.

I can't describe the terror of having absolutely no choice how I looked or behaved. Though the truth about my life has been blurred, I wasn't an immoral woman or a bad person—just crazy! My malady was not genetic or learned. It was demons. I wanted to die.

That is, until Jesus came to me. He called them demons. He spoke to them, rebuked them, and sent them running! In that moment, I was gloriously set free and my new life began.

Returning to Magdala was never an option. From that first meeting, I knew I could never bring myself to walk away from Jesus. And so, I stayed—following Him, supporting, and learning from Him. I remember the day I heard Him explain what it meant to be a true follower. "If anyone would come after me, he must deny himself and take up his cross and follow me."[1]

Well, I would have gladly carried His cross the day of His Crucifixion—if anyone had let me. There was nothing I could do to ease His pain, but I was there. I stayed.

I remember thinking: *Can You see my face Jesus? Have I ever told You how much I love You, how grateful I am to You? Have I ever mentioned how in awe I am of Your compassion, Your vulnerability as both God and man, Your unconditional love? Jesus, I'm sorry. It's so hard to watch. To see Your tortured expression as You are stripped and exposed to the elements. To hear the hammer strike the nails in Your hands and feet. To smell Your sweat and blood.*

That's why the only person I absolutely did not expect to see that morning was Jesus. The burial had been hurried because of the Sabbath. But I knew one last thing I could do for Him—one last way Mary and Salome and I could express our love. We would return to the tomb and give Jesus' body a proper burial.

What happened next is blurry—a powerful earthquake, an angel of the Lord telling us not to panic, and then the words that turned our terror to pure joy. "He is not here; he has been brought back to life as He said. Come see the place where He was lying."

I grabbed Salome and Mary by their hands and squeezed tight. Suddenly, it all made sense. We had seen Jesus being manhandled by sinners. We had stayed and watched every dreadful minute, for six long hours. And now—the third day—today! He must be raised

---

[1]Matthew 16:24.

from the dead. The tomb was empty. Empty!

"Master, it's you!" That's all I could say when Jesus met us on our way from the tomb to tell His disciples what happened. We collapsed at His feet. Jesus said, "You're holding on to me for dear life! Don't be frightened like that. Go tell my brothers they are to go to Galilee, and that I'll meet them there."

My joy is impossible to contain. When Jesus lovingly said my name it was not "mad Mary." It was simply, "Mary."

Is it any wonder that I love Him? He delivered me. His Spirit strengthens and keeps me. He granted me the honor of being the first person to spread the Good News about His Resurrection.

My life has meaning simply because I stayed.

EMBRACING THE PENTECOSTAL PERSPECTIVE
What is the Holy Spirit teaching me?

Nicodemus and Mary Magdalene give us wonderful pictures of the journey of faith. We see both of them in their lives before Christ—one blinded by religion and the other by demonic possession. Then we fast forward to the foot of the Cross—an important and frequent intersection for living faith—and find them again (Luke 23:55, John 19:39), acting out of love for their Lord. What was it that kept their faith vibrant and growing from the starting point?

One common factor is *wonder*. Nicodemus's curiosity led him to seek the Lord. *I wonder what makes Him different? I wonder what it means to be born again?* It seems likely, especially when we read of Paul's insatiable desire to know the Lord (Philippians 3:10), that this curiosity never ceased. May we always have the freedom to ask honest questions and find life-changing answers.

Mary's wonder —a sense of awe—stemmed from an encounter with His amazing love and power. While she grew away from her old life, she never forgot or took for granted the incredible freedom Jesus gave her with the gracious gift of salvation. Such wonder is cultivated by the Holy Spirit and by improving our powers of observation—looking for God not only in our personal lives but also in creation and in others.

What questions have you asked the Lord lately? Do you ask Jesus directly or only others?

How do you keep your wonder fresh concerning the things of God?

Secondly, Nicodemus and Mary shared an obvious hunger for the things of God. Nicodemus recognized the famine of faith in his Pharisaical experience, so he met with Jesus in the hope of finding more. Mary took the extraordinary step of leaving behind her previous life and following Jesus (Luke 8:2,3).

How can the world take the edge off your hunger for God?

How do you increase your appetite for the things of God?

Finally, as we encounter Nicodemus and Mary Magdalene at the Cross, one thing is evident about their quality of faith: It is not diminished by either hard times or lack of understanding. Oftentimes, these two go together. We suffer something difficult and we wonder where God is, or how He could allow it, or what good it could possibly accomplish. Yet these faithful friends show us just exactly how we should respond at such times. We should press in close to the Lord, continue to follow Him, serve as best we can with our limited understanding, and wait patiently for further revelation. Like Nicodemus and Mary, we will likely find courage, conviction, boldness, and perseverance born of the Spirit.

Share a personal, faith-shaking experience.

Nicodemus had fellowship with Joseph of Arimathea, and Mary was in the company of other women. **In addition to the ever-present Holy Spirit, who do you walk with in your faith journey?**

INVITING GOD TO CHANGE MY VIEW
What change is God asking me to make?

Many movies and television shows are built around the saga of a growing love relationship emphasizing the couple's dating life. The plot inevitably culminates in the engagement, declaration of love, or wedding of the couple. Rarely does a story line successfully continue past this point.

Sometimes we make the same mistake in Christianity with an overemphasis on the beginning of one's relationship with Jesus. The Lord does not lose interest in us once we come to Him. He desires us to have a living, vibrant faith, one that explores what it means to follow Him closely.

Where are you on your faith journey: playing the field (considering many faiths), dating exclusively (committed to learning more about Jesus), newly married (new believer), or married for a period of time (walking with the Lord)? How can we pray for you at this stage of your walk?

Has your faith been tested by difficulty recently? What do you need to sense God's love for you? Would you like to confess a lack of hunger for the things of God?

Prayer

Heavenly Father, I am so encouraged by the testimonies of Your servants Nicodemus and Mary Magdalene, coming to you from two different extremes. Surely with You there is room for each person. Thank You for making Your divine love evident to me in a thousand ways, the greatest of which was to send Your own Son to die on the Cross. I rejoice in His Resurrection and pray that You will resurrect within me a faith so vibrant, that it reflects the beauty of Your wonderful love. I want to know You, serve You, follow You, and love You more than ever before. In Your precious name I ask this, Amen.

JOURNALING

Take a few minutes to record your personal insights from the lesson.

Her *Vital Community*

CATCHING SIGHT
Introduction

*A*NTICIPATION WAS HIGH—the night had finally arrived for Sue to be baptized. The pastor was already in the baptismal tank, the new converts were lined up, and the worship team had just finished singing. Pastor raised his hand and motioned to Sue that it was time to begin. Imagine everyone's surprise when she dove head first into the baptismal tank! Sue had missed the instructional meeting. But she knew exactly what being baptized symbolized.

For the past five years, Sue had been in and out of rehab centers trying to free herself from the addiction of cocaine. Nothing seemed to work. One night a friend invited her to a concert where an invitation was given for individuals to accept Jesus—to make Him Lord of their lives. Sue made a decision that night to give God a chance.

When the roots of plants form connections, a substance is present that strengthens all of the plants. This fungus, called *mycorrhizae,* helps link roots of different plants—even of dissimilar species. If one plant has access to water, another to nutrients, and a third to sunshine, they all have the means to share with one another.

Like the trees and other plants in a forest, Christians in the church, especially new Christians like Sue, need one another for support and growth.

GETTING FOCUSED

Begin your study by considering the following:

A healthy Christian community attracts people to Christ. What are you doing to make your church the kind of place that will attract others to Christ?

BIBLE READING

Matthew 3:13–15; Luke 22:17–20; Acts 2:42–47

New International Version

Matthew 3:13 Then Jesus came from Galilee to the Jordan to be baptized by John. 14 But John tried to deter him, saying, "I need to be baptized by you, and do you come to me?"

15 Jesus replied, "Let it be so now; it is proper for us to do this to fulfill all righteousness." Then John consented.

Luke 22:17 After taking the cup, he [Jesus] gave thanks and said, "Take this and divide it among you. 18 For I tell you I will not drink again of the fruit of the vine until the kingdom of God comes."

19 And he took bread, gave thanks and broke it, and gave it to them, saying, "This is my body given for you; do this in remembrance of me."

20 In the same way, after the supper he took the cup, saying, "This cup is the new covenant in my blood, which is poured out for you."

Acts 2:42 They devoted themselves to the apostles' teaching and

New Living Translation

Matthew 3:13 Then Jesus went from Galilee to the Jordan River to be baptized by John. 14 But John didn't want to baptize him. "I am the one who needs to be baptized by you," he said, "so why are you coming to me?"

15 But Jesus said, "It must be done, because we must do everything that is right." So then John baptized him.

Luke 22:17 Then he [Jesus] took a cup of wine, and when he had given thanks for it, he said, "Take this and share it among yourselves. 18 For I will not drink wine again until the Kingdom of God has come."

19 Then he took a loaf of bread; and when he had thanked God for it, he broke it in pieces and gave it to the disciples, saying, "This is my body, given for you. Do this in remembrance of me." 20 After supper he took another cup of wine and said, "This wine is the token of God's new covenant to save you— an agreement sealed with the blood

New International Version

to the fellowship, to the breaking of bread and to prayer. 43 Everyone was filled with awe, and many wonders and miraculous signs were done by the apostles. 44 All the believers were together and had everything in common. 45 Selling their possessions and goods, they gave to anyone as he had need. 46 Every day they continued to meet together in the temple courts. They broke bread in their homes and ate together with glad and sincere hearts, 47 praising God and enjoying the favor of all the people. And the Lord added to their number daily those who were being saved.

New Living Translation

I will pour out for you."

Acts 2:42 They joined with the other believers and devoted themselves to the apostles' teaching and fellowship, sharing in the Lord's Supper and in prayer.

43 A deep sense of awe came over them all, and the apostles performed many miraculous signs and wonders. 44 And all the believers met together constantly and shared everything they had. 45 They sold their possessions and shared the proceeds with those in need. 46 They worshiped together at the Temple each day, met in homes for the Lord's Supper, and shared their meals with great joy and generosity —47 all the while praising God and enjoying the goodwill of all the people. And each day the Lord added to their group those who were being saved.

GAINING BIBLICAL INSIGHT
Identifying with God's people

Waiting without knowing was the hardest part. Jesus had not said what would happen, He had only said to wait to receive power. How that power would come or what would happen afterward they did not know, but the disciples patiently waited in faith.

Suddenly, after long days of waiting, a rushing sound like wind from heaven pierced the silence of the Upper Room. A holy presence invigorated the disciples who may have been weary from waiting. Without question, they knew this was what they were waiting for. The Holy Spirit had come.

Sharing in the Christian Community

Jesus told the disciples He would build His Church but He did not explain, or define it. However, after the Day of Pentecost, the believers from the Upper Room and those who joined them gathered in Christian communities which became known as the Church. They continued living in their own homes, but they spent as much time as possible with other Christians in a caring community. Today, the universal Church is the body of believers all over the world; the local church is a group of believers in the same geographic area.

Being involved with a community of believers is vital for anyone desiring to live the life of faith. Though becoming a Christian is an individual choice, the Christian life is never lived in isolation. It is always found in relationship to a community of believers.

Read Acts 2:42. What were the chief reasons the community of believers came together?

According to this passage believers came together for fellowship to strengthen and encourage their faith. The apostles taught the Scriptures, the foundation for faith, and believers joined in prayer and worship. The functions of this community—teaching, praying, sharing in fellowship—are still the chief functions of the Church today.

As you read about this first community of believers, what characteristics do you see that you could expect to find in a twenty-first century church?

A church is different from any other social group. People from vastly different walks of life gather with a common purpose. The presence of the Holy Spirit blends them in an atmosphere of love expressed in many ways. Luke describes the generosity, unity, and sincerity of these believers as well as their gratitude to God for His blessings. Jesus said the mark of believers would be their love for God and man. That love, evident in this Early Church, is still available as yielded believers respond to the Spirit.

Committing to the Christian Community

From the time of Christ, water baptism has been the mark of committing to Christ and the Christian community. Paul describes the act of going under the water and being raised out of the water as a symbol of the death and resurrection of Christ.

Jesus emphasized the importance of water baptism by both example and teaching. His own water baptism was a public demonstration of His commitment to God. Though He was sinless, He identified with humanity and set the example for others to follow.

Read the account of Jesus' personal baptism in Matthew 3:13–15. **In what way do you see water baptism as symbolic of the death and resurrection of Christ?**

Jesus' last instruction to His disciples was to go into the world and make disciples of all nations by teaching and baptizing. In cultures without Christian influence, declaring Christian faith by being baptized in water may alienate some believers from family and friends. In spite of this, water baptism has remained through the centuries as the lasting symbol of identifying with the Christian community, an outward acknowledgement of the inward work of grace.

Celebrating with the Christian Community

While water baptism is a means of declaring the beginning of the Christian life, sharing in the Lord's table celebrates the continuing relationship with the Christian community. Jesus instituted this observance, called Communion, the night before His crucifixion.

Read the account of the Last Supper in Luke 22:14–20. What do you think the Lord was feeling at this time?

As Jesus approached His death, He and His disciples celebrated the Jewish Passover. Departing from the usual statements accompanying the meal, Jesus declared the bread as symbolic of His body which would be broken and the wine as symbolic of the new covenant of His blood.

The apostle Paul later referred to these words of Jesus when instructing the Early Church to keep communion as a twofold celebration. First, it is a memorial of Christ's death, and second, a reminder of His future return.

This celebration of Communion is to be kept periodically, with no scriptural instructions as to exactly how often. It is not to be an empty ritual, carried out dutifully, but a joyful ceremony rich in meaning, showing the relationship of the believer with Christ. While we look back to the Cross and forward to His return, sharing the symbols of His body and His blood also has meaning for the present as a reminder of the closeness of our identity with Him. In every

Communion service we reaffirm our relationship with Christ.

Salvation is by faith in the work of Christ on the Cross. Water baptism is the outward expression of our faith, declaring our identity with the Christian community with which we share fellowship and the study of God's Word. Regularly participating in Communion at the Lord's table affirms our commitment to Him until He comes. Being in fellowship with a Christian community is vital to the continuation of our faith walk.

Lydia, an influential businesswoman in Philippi, became a believer in Christ as a result of Paul's teaching in a meeting on a riverbank. Immediately she declared her faith by water baptism and fellowshipping with the believers. Let's hear her story.

REFLECTING HIS IMAGE
Lydia (Acts 16:13–15; 1 Timothy 6:17,18)

There are not enough hours in this day, Lydia thought. Examining the exquisite blue to red fabric before her, keen eyes and delicate fingers assured her the purple silk would bring a handsome price. Royal dignitaries throughout Philippi—the perfect place for cultured and affluent women—were the reason things were going well. Only the very rich could afford her merchandise.

No doubt about it. Lydia was a woman of means and status; a successful businesswoman and the head of a household. She knew how to make a living on her own.

Sighing wearily now, Lydia yawned and looked out at the setting sun. Her thoughts wandered from fine cloth to her new Christian friends.

The words of Paul from weeks earlier still captivated her. Already a worshiper of God, she was a Gentile. And though not a full convert to Judaism, she studied the Jewish faith with fervency and passion.

Suddenly, her thoughts found her sitting by the river with friends—other believing women who had come to worship God under the open sky and near the running water. Lydia became pensive as she saw the events of that day again through her mind's eye.

"Look," one of the women said. "Over there. That man is talking to Anna, Dorcas, and Rebecca. See how they sit and listen to him."

Moments later, Lydia slowly walked to the circle that had formed. Her friends sat silent, and looked as if they were searching for understanding of the truth and profoundness of what had just been said. *This conversation runs deeper than an idle stream of thought,* she reasoned.

She listened as Paul spoke of Jesus. And as she listened to the good news, the Holy Spirit opened her heart and mind to Paul's message.

"Do you understand?" Paul asked them all. Quiet reigned in that moment. Lydia made a decision of her own. Swallowing hard, she stood to her feet. "I understand," she said, "and I believe."

Lydia listened for more than an hour as Paul and the other men continued to teach about Jesus' life, death, and Resurrection and how water baptism for the true follower is a symbol of the believer's burial and resurrection with Christ. And again she responded, this time through her own baptism.

Glowing with the love of God as she was raised from the water, she knew in an instant that in spite of her self-sufficiency she had found something she needed—something outside herself.

She said, "If you're confident that I'm in this with you and believe in the Master truly, come home with me and be my guests"[1] The men hesitated, but Lydia wouldn't take no for an answer.

As they sat waiting for the evening meal to be served, one of the men spoke. "Your generosity and hospitality are unique gifts God can use for provision to the church." Lydia knew days like this would be the first of many cherished memories.

Now, as a long day was drawing to an end, she sat down to fold the last stack of polished cloth and to offer a simple prayer. *Jesus, my life changed forever that day by the river because I found You. Use my home for Your glory, to bring rest and comfort to the weary.*

Through the years Lydia would grow in her faith and learn more about what her friend Paul meant when he said "those who are rich in this present world [are] . . . to do good, to be rich in good deeds, and to be generous and willing to share."[2]

---

[1] Acts 16:15, *The Message.*
[2] 1 Timothy 6:17,18.

EMBRACING THE PENTECOSTAL PERSPECTIVE
What is the Holy Spirit teaching me?

We owe a debt of gratitude to Lydia. Her testimony reminds us that the Church is not a place but a divine community. She discovered it on the banks of a river, then cultivated it in her own home—never trying to contain it, only to participate in it. Too often today, church is a place where we hold membership, park in familiar territory (cars and bodies!), speak to a select group of people, check in and out of with some regularity, and, sometimes, trade for a different model. God intended so much more.

He calls us to a fresh experience of love, joy, renewal, and purpose, all while in the company of others who are equally imperfect. You may never encounter a more diverse group of people, yet you will marvel at the unity available through God's Spirit. When peace is sparse, the enemy's activity obvious, and our own weaknesses abundant, is it any wonder God's Word clearly warns believers not to forsake His Church?

Do you attend church regularly? Why or why not?

Which things named above have to do with the blessings of God's community, rather than the superficial values of our culture?

God asks us to live changed lives through the power of the Holy Spirit. This transformation cannot, should not, be hidden. Instead, we mark the start of our journey with the public testimony of baptism and validate that identity every day with our actions.

How can we capture and carry the essence of water baptism—a demonstration of our new life in Christ—in our everyday lives?

If someone expressed hesitation about the importance or even the necessity of being baptized, how would you respond?

Peter graphically describes the life of Jesus on earth as a template over which we may lay our own lives (1 Peter 2:21). The Early Church, including the first disciples as well as others like Lydia who soon followed after, retraced that pattern with bold markings. Celebrating the Lord's Supper is one of those essential acts. No matter what your upbringing, Communion can and should be a very meaningful experience.

What does celebrating the Lord's Supper highlight concerning your spiritual life?

How would you celebrate Communion to better reflect the community of Christ, rather than an individual act?

INVITING GOD TO CHANGE MY VIEW
What change is God asking me to make?

In the 2004 Summer Olympics in Athens, highlighted by many wonderful stories of courage and spirit as well as tragedy and disappointment, one account stands out. A young U.S. athlete was just one shot from the gold medal in the three position rifle competition. He carefully took aim, steadied himself, and fired. It was an admirable effort, well within the range needed to secure the gold, and yet the judges awarded him a zero for that shot. Stunned, as were most of the onlookers, the competitor learned that he had cross-fired, lining up with the wrong target!

When left to our own skills and intelligence, we inevitably miss the mark. God, in His gracious wisdom, provides a community of believers to help safeguard against that possibility.

Are you serving the Lord faithfully in a local church? Do you need the courage to proclaim your faith publicly through water baptism? If you still feel disconnected at your church, name one way you could meet people. Or think of someone you know who may feel disconnected, and invite them to join you in attending a service.

Prayer
Father, thank You for drawing me into Your family. I am affirmed by Your Spirit as I acknowledge the greatness of Your Church and what it cost Your Son to secure my place in Your family. Now, aligned with Your people and purpose, I am energized by the vision of making an eternal contribution. I am Your daughter. Your Church is my family. You are my Lord. Amen.

JOURNALING

Take a few minutes to record your personal insights from the lesson.

Her Deepening Spirituality

CATCHING SIGHT

Introduction

A SMALL BOY BEGAN to cry after falling out of his bed. His mother rushed into his room and asked him what happened. "I guess I got too close to where I got in," he replied. Too many Christians may do just that. They actually repent of their sins—an excellent beginning—but they stay too close to "where they got in."

As we share the gospel, our goal should not be merely to see others profess faith or begin attending church, but to see them mature in their faith. Spiritual growth is a continual, gradual process.

After years of marriage a couple can read each other's nonverbal communication very well. A variety of "those looks" can say so much. The look can say, "I'm proud of you," or "I've heard that story before, and it sounded different this time." Just as "that look" from a spouse can convey messages to us, we need to understand that the closer we get to our Master the easier it is for Him to convey His pleasure or displeasure with us. Through this lesson we can understand that Jesus desires for us to have an intimate relationship with Him. However, we also need to desire a close relationship with Him.

GETTING FOCUSED

Begin your study by considering the following:

What changes have you noticed in your life since becoming a Christian? Have those changes helped you develop a closer relationship with Jesus?

BIBLE READING

John 15:1–11, 15–17

New International Version

1 "I am the true vine, and my Father is the gardener. 2 He cuts off every branch in me that bears no fruit, while every branch that does bear fruit he prunes so that it will be even more fruitful. 3 You are already clean because of the word I have spoken to you. 4 Remain in me, and I will remain in you. No branch can bear fruit by itself; it must remain in the vine. Neither can you bear fruit unless you remain in me.

5 "I am the vine; you are the branches. If a man remains in me and I in him, he will bear much fruit; apart from me you can do nothing. 6 If anyone does not remain in me, he is like a branch that is thrown away and withers; such branches are picked up, thrown into the fire and burned. 7 If you remain in me and my words remain in you, ask whatever you wish, and it will be given you. 8 This is to my Father's glory, that you bear much fruit, showing

New Living Translation

1 "I am the true vine, and my Father is the gardener. 2 He cuts off every branch that doesn't produce fruit, and he prunes the branches that do bear fruit so they will produce even more. 3 You have already been pruned for greater fruitfulness by the message I have given you. 4 Remain in me, and I will remain in you. For a branch cannot produce fruit if it is severed from the vine, and you cannot be fruitful apart from me.

5 "Yes, I am the vine; you are the branches. Those who remain in me, and I in them, will produce much fruit. For apart from me you can do nothing. 6 Anyone who parts from me is thrown away like a useless branch and withers. Such branches are gathered into a pile to be burned. 7 But if you stay joined to me and my words remain in you, you may ask any request you like, and it will be granted! 8 My true disciples produce much fruit. This brings great glory to my Father.

New International Version

yourselves to be my disciples.

9 "As the Father has loved me, so have I loved you. Now remain in my love. 10 If you obey my commands, you will remain in my love, just as I have obeyed my Father's commands and remain in his love. 11 I have told you this so that my joy may be in you and that your joy may be complete.

15 "I no longer call you servants, because a servant does not know his master's business. Instead, I have called you friends, for everything that I learned from my Father I have made known to you. 16 You did not choose me, but I chose you and appointed you to go and bear fruit—fruit that will last. Then the Father will give you whatever you ask in my name. 17 This is my command: Love each other."

New Living Translation

9 "I have loved you even as the Father has loved me. Remain in my love. 10 When you obey me, you remain in my love, just as I obey my Father and remain in his love. 11 I have told you this so that you will be filled with my joy. Yes, your joy will overflow!

15 "I no longer call you servants, because a master doesn't confide in his servants. Now you are my friends, since I have told you everything the Father told me. 16 You didn't choose me. I chose you. I appointed you to go and produce fruit that will last, so that the Father will give you whatever you ask for, using my name. 17 I command you to love each other."

GAINING BIBLICAL INSIGHT
Building intimacy with my Savior

The table conversation had been sobering. The traditional Passover meal had taken some unfamiliar turns. First, Jesus surprised everyone by washing their feet, an act usually performed by a servant. He shocked them later by saying someone would betray Him, that even Peter would deny Him. Jesus also disturbed them by saying He would not keep Passover again because He was going away. But the meal finally ended and it was time to go to the Mount of Olives.

Jesus may have begun talking seriously as He looked out a window at the tendrils of a vine, or waited until they could see the vineyards near the Mount of Olives. Perhaps thinking of the impending betrayal of Judas and the denial of Peter, He emphasized the importance of staying connected with Him.

Living in Relationship with Christ

Jesus knew the next few hours would physically separate the disciples from Him. He wanted them to know His love for them would continue, that they should rest securely in that love.

The disciples understood disconnectedness. They had seen branches wither after being cut off. They knew vitality depended on remaining connected to the living vine.

Jesus instructed, "Live in Me. Make your home in Me just as I do in you." The disciples must have been puzzled as they heard these words because Jesus had just told them He was going away. *How could they live in Him?* Later they would understand He was talking about spiritual unity which all believers experience when they receive Him into their lives.

What implications does "Make your home in Me" have for believers?

A good home is a place of security and acceptance—a place where lives are shaped, the launching pad for interaction in the community. In a good home, needs are met, physically and emotionally. It is the warm, loving refuge from a cold, unfriendly world.

Jesus offers this kind of relationship to believers. The one condition is continuing in Him. "Remain in Me," Jesus told them. "I am here for you, but you must stay with Me."

Growing in Knowledge of Christ through His Word

The next few hours would bring severe tests for the disciples. Though Jesus had tried to tell them what was coming, they did not understand it. When the Cross brought physical separation from Him, they had to ponder His words.

Our perspective is different than the disciples' because we know the outcome of these events. We have the written Word of God and the Holy Spirit as our Teacher. The message is the same, however, as it was to the disciples that night: To remain in Christ, His Word must remain in us.

Gaining understanding of the Word of God is much more than an intellectual activity. Through our knowledge of the Word of God we grow in a joyful relationship with Jesus. Gaining factual knowledge of the Word is a means to that end. Our purpose is always to deepen our relationship with Jesus through our increased knowledge of His Word.

What method of Bible study have you found helpful in your pursuit of biblical knowledge?

Methods of gaining scriptural knowledge may vary from topical studies to whole book studies. Sometimes we may read lengthy portions of Scripture; other times we may concentrate for long periods on a passage. The method of study is not as important as the manner. Consistent Bible study with mind and heart open to what the Spirit is saying through the Word is a means of making ourselves at home in Christ's love.

Developing Intimacy with Christ through Prayer

Jesus referred to another dimension of the disciples' relationship with Him: communication in prayer. Continuing the imagery of the vine, Jesus spoke about the disciples' future. "Just as vines bear fruit, your lives will bear evidence of your relationship with Me," He said, "and this kind of living will bring glory to the Father." The ongoing relationship with Christ includes communication through prayer, which results in fruitfulness.

The disciples were familiar with Jesus' prayer life. They knew He rose early to spend hours talking with His Father. They heard the short prayer at Lazarus' tomb. Prayer was such a vital part of His life, they had asked Him to teach them to pray. This brief reference to prayer was a continuation of that teaching.

What conditions did Jesus place on prayer at this time, according to verse 7?

The emphasis of this passage is on the relationship between Jesus and the disciples. He talked about the love of the Father and the love the disciples should have for each other. He talked about joy as an outgrowth of these relationships. He called the disciples His friends, because of the closeness of His relationship to them.

In this context, prayer is communication between friends. "You know My heart, you live in My Word. What can I do for you that would bring glory to the Father?" is the essence of what He said. "The Father will act because of your relationship with Me."

This brief teaching on prayer helps us so much in our private devotional life. The most intimate thoughts may be shared with Jesus. Our prayers are sincere expressions of our hearts, couched in the simplest of terms. This kind of prayer, an outgrowth of our relationship with Christ and His Word, is the means for developing intimacy with our Savior.

Hannah was a woman who knew much about prayer. She prayed in the face of ridicule and misunderstanding. She shared the deepest feelings of her heart in prayer to the Lord. His answer brought joy to her heart and a smile to her face. Let's hear her story.

REFLECTING HIS IMAGE
Hannah (1 Samuel 1:1 to 2:21)

Yesterday I took a walk. It couldn't have taken more than an hour. I passed familiar trees and houses and faces. I passed by a group of children playing and laughing together. On my walk—my prayer time with the Lord—I remembered the grief and the joy of the past. And in remembering, I wept. I walked and I wept.

You see, I couldn't have children. And to make matters worse, my husband's other wife, Penninah, ridiculed me on a daily basis, rubbing it in and never letting me forget. "Such a pity," she would say as she looked right through me. "I can't imagine how empty and incomplete you must feel."

I looked into *her* eyes and I got angry. Her condescension wounded me and caused me to want to hide from friends, family, and God. And it was the same, day after day, year after year.

How my arms ached to hold a baby of my own.

"Hannah, don't cry," my husband would say. "It doesn't matter to me. I love you. And besides, am I not more to you than ten sons?"

Of course, Elkanah mattered immensely. But his words did little to console me. Penninah gave him children. I could not.

I don't remember the exact day I began my daily walk to talk to God. But seeing those children playing yesterday reminded me of God's faithfulness and of the day I became convinced He met me *as* I was *where* I was.

The priest Eli was on duty at the entrance to God's temple the day I came to pray. I covered my face, fell to my knees, and called out to God in a way I never had before. Rocking back and forth, my soul

felt crushed at the thought of another passing day without a child!
 Right then and there I made a promise.

> "Oh GOD-of-the-Angel-Armies,
> If you'll take a good hard look at my pain,
> If you'll quit neglecting me and go into action for me
> By giving me a son,
> I'll give him completely, unreservedly to you.
> I'll set him apart for a life of holy discipline."[1]

Eli was watching me. As he approached, I knew from his look of disdain that he misunderstood my pain. He actually thought I was drunk! But prayer is effective and loaded with grace.[2] I explained myself and he blessed me. Filled with relief and hope, I got up, washed my face and decided to eat.

Soon I conceived and my boy was born. Talk about ultimate joy! I cried as the women examined and cleaned my son. "Does he have a name?" one of them asked.

"Yes. Yes, he has a name," I said as I choked back emotion. "His name is Samuel, which means 'asked of the LORD.' "

Seven years ago God gave Elkanah and me a beautiful, healthy son. I'm still praising and thanking Him for answering my prayer. I've kept my promise. Samuel lives at the temple in Shiloh.

I miss my son, but I know how to handle the pain of his absence. I pray. And every year I sew and deliver a new robe for him. Every stitch in that robe represents a prayer for him.

For, you see, prayer is more than enough when you are confronted with an overwhelming circumstance. More than enough. It unlocks the presence and power of God himself.[3]

I wanted to tell you about my walk just in case you feel like running away from a taunting voice whose words seek to devour and destroy you. Just in case you're at a breaking point. Just in case you can't see any way you'll make it another day.

Hold on. Talk to God.

---

[1] 1 Samuel 1:11, *The Message.*
[2] Jean E. Syswerda, ed., *Women of Faith Study Bible*, New International Version (Grand Rapids: Zondervan Corporation, 2001), 739.
[3] Ibid.

EMBRACING THE PENTECOSTAL PERSPECTIVE
What is the Holy Spirit teaching me?

One glorious fall day, while walking through a state park, a hiker discovered a large hanging vine at one end of a wide dip in the trail. Doing her best jungle-woman imitation, she swung joyfully from one side of the trail's "chasm" to the other. But suddenly the hiker found herself airborne. What had begun as a brilliant display of strength and grace ended abruptly with an ignominious drop to the forest floor. Apparently, her vine-swinging talents had very little depth.

Such is the experience of many believers who begin walking with their Savior. Grafted onto the True Vine, Jesus Christ, we enjoy the initial thrill of forgiveness. Dropping the burden of sin fills our hearts with gravity-defying joy and we soar in excitement. Then we encounter a difficulty, drop our Savior's hand, revert to the old habit of self-reliance, and find ourselves with nowhere to go but down.

Jesus invites us not only to connect with Him but to develop and grow in that connection. The vine is a powerful illustration of intimacy and life. Hannah reminds us that life is simply too difficult to handle on our own. Why would we even want to try?

What are the biggest hindrances to developing intimacy with your Savior?

One of our most common frustrations in building intimacy with Christ is the lack of visible interaction. Hannah could relate. She trusted God, she served Him faithfully, but her arms remained empty. She wanted to believe for the desire of her heart, but the emptiness threatened to overwhelm her.

Thankfully, God gave us a very powerful, tangible witness. We can reach out and touch His Word. It is the life-giving flow of nutrition from Him to us. Reading, studying, memorizing, and meditating on the Bible should not be a chore so much as the easiest point of connection to Him.

God promises that we will have the Spirit's help in understanding His Word (1 Corinthians 2:12–14). **Do you invite the Holy Spirit to bring illumination?**

Hannah's experience of prevailing prayer inspires us. We will all stand at the brink of a chasm that is too wide, deep, or treacherous for us to cross in our own ability. An intimate relationship with Jesus will minimize the intimidation of that moment, and we will find the strength to take the situation to God.

When you don't know how to pray, do you allow the Holy Spirit to pray through you? (Romans 8:26)

INVITING GOD TO CHANGE MY VIEW
What change is God asking me to make?

A child, weeding the garden, accidentally uprooted a vegetable plant. Hoping that no one would notice, she replanted it, believing that it would take root again. It seemed only moments later, however, that the plant drooped, completely negating the charade the child had so carefully arranged.

Eventually the child learned that merely giving the appearance of life was not going to fool anyone—least of all the plant! All living things require consistent connection to nutrients and water. Humans are no different, physically or spiritually. We must abide *in* the Vine.

Self-determination, unproductive guilt, and vain hope disconnected from action will never build an intimate relationship with our Savior. Confession, dependence on the Holy Spirit, and stirring our hunger for Jesus will build the relationship we desire with Him.

Do you want to confess your desire to grow closer to your Savior? How, specifically, do you want to see your prayer life improve? What kind of interaction with God's Word would you like to experience in the next six months? Do you need to begin a relationship with Jesus today?

Prayer
Heavenly Father, thank You for drawing near to me. I want to draw near to You, too. I'm not sure I understand all our relationship can be, but I'm willing to trust that You will show me. I pray for greater under-standing as I read Your Word and deeper conversations when I spend time in prayer. Restrain me, by Your Spirit, from ever just going through the motions. I am not willing to settle for a polite friendship with Jesus. Help me to learn what it means to abide in the Vine. I pray in the name of my Lord, Amen.

JOURNALING
Take a few minutes to record your personal insights from the lesson.

Her Enduring Empowerment

CATCHING SIGHT
Introduction

WITH A FLICK OF the fingers, friction occurs and a spark leaps from match to kindling. A small flame burns the edges and grows, fueled by wood and air. Heat builds, and soon flames lick the kindling. Higher and wider the flames spread, consuming the wood. The flame has become a fire.

Over two thousand years ago, a match was struck in Jerusalem. At first, just a few in that corner of the world were touched; but the fire spread beyond Jerusalem out to the world and to all people. The apostle Peter was changed the day that flame reached him. Peter, who had denied he even knew Jesus at the time of Jesus' final trial and crucifixion, was able to speak boldly after the Day of Pentecost.

As with all aspects of the Christian life, living in the fullness of the Spirit can only be accomplished through a daily walk of faith. During this lesson, put yourself in the place of the disciples—feel with them as they are filled with the Holy Spirit, and thrill with them as they see thousands respond to the gospel message. Watch the Spirit-led boldness of these first-century believers. Then decide to be a twenty-first century version of those men and women of God.

GETTING FOCUSED

Begin your study by considering the following:

If you have experienced the baptism in the Holy Spirit, share that experience with others in your group.

BIBLE READING

Matthew 3:11; Acts 1:8; 2:1–4; 10:44–46; 19:4–7; Galatians 5:16–18

New International Version

Matthew 3:11 "I baptize you with water for repentance. But after me will come one who is more powerful than I, whose sandals I am not fit to carry. He will baptize you with the Holy Spirit and with fire."

Acts 1:8 "But you will receive power when the Holy Spirit comes on you; and you will be my witnesses in Jerusalem, and in all Judea and Samaria, and to the ends of the earth."

2:1 When the day of Pentecost came, they were all together in one place. 2 Suddenly a sound like the blowing of a violent wind came from heaven and filled the whole house where they were sitting. 3 They saw what seemed to be tongues of fire that separated and came to rest on each of them. 4 All of them were filled with the Holy Spirit and began to speak in other tongues as the Spirit enabled them.

10:44 While Peter was still speaking these words, the Holy Spirit came on all who heard the message. 45 The circumcised believers who had come with Peter were astonished that the gift of the Holy Spirit

New Living Translation

Matthew 3:11 "I baptize with water those who turn from their sins and turn to God. But someone is coming soon who is far greater than I am—so much greater that I am not even worthy to be his slave. He will baptize you with the Holy Spirit and with fire."

Acts 1:8 "But when the Holy Spirit has come upon you, you will receive power and will tell people about me everywhere—in Jerusalem, throughout Judea, in Samaria, and to the ends of the earth."

2:1 On the day of Pentecost, seven weeks after Jesus' resurrection, the believers were meeting together in one place. 2 Suddenly, there was a sound from heaven like the roaring of a mighty windstorm in the skies above them, and it filled the house where they were meeting. 3 Then, what looked like flames or tongues of fire appeared and settled on each of them. 4 And everyone present was filled with the Holy Spirit and began speaking in other languages, as the Holy Spirit gave them this ability.

New International Version

had been poured out even on the Gentiles. 46 For they heard them speaking in tongues and praising God.

19:4 Paul said, "John's baptism was a baptism of repentance. He told the people to believe in the one coming after him, that is, in Jesus." 5 On hearing this, they were baptized into the name of the Lord Jesus. 6 When Paul placed his hands on them, the Holy Spirit came on them, and they spoke in tongues and prophesied. 7 There were about twelve men in all.

Galatians 5:16 So I say, live by the Spirit, and you will not gratify the desires of the sinful nature. 17 For the sinful nature desires what is contrary to the Spirit, and the Spirit what is contrary to the sinful nature. They are in conflict with each other, so that you do not do what you want. 18 But if you are led by the Spirit, you are not under law.

New Living Translation

10:44 Even as Peter was saying these things, the Holy Spirit fell upon all who had heard the message. 45 The Jewish believers who came with Peter were amazed that the gift of the Holy Spirit had been poured out upon the Gentiles, too. 46 And there could be no doubt about it, for they heard them speaking in tongues and praising God.

19:4 Paul said, "John's baptism was to demonstrate a desire to turn from sin and turn to God. John himself told the people to believe in Jesus, the one John said would come later." 5 As soon as they heard this, they were baptized in the name of the Lord Jesus. 6 Then when Paul laid his hands on them, the Holy Spirit came on them, and they spoke in other tongues and prophesied. 7 There were about twelve men in all.

Galatians 5:16 So I advise you to live according to your new life in the Holy Spirit. Then you won't be doing what your sinful nature craves. 17 The old sinful nature loves to do evil, which is just opposite from what the Holy Spirit wants. And the Spirit gives us desires that are opposite from what the sinful nature desires. These two forces are constantly fighting each other, and your choices are never free from this conflict. 18 But when you are directed by the Holy Spirit, you are no longer subject to the law.

GAINING BIBLICAL INSIGHT
Experiencing the reality of the Holy Spirit

*I*srael had not had a prophet for more than four hundred years when the thunderous John the Baptist appeared. His fiery message of repentance filled people with awe. They waited expectantly for him to announce he was the Christ, but John assured them he was not. Instead he prophesied that Christ would baptize with the Holy Spirit. This prophecy was not fulfilled during Jesus' earthly ministry, but after His return to His Father.

Anticipating the Spirit's Coming

Imagine yourself standing on the banks of the Jordan River listening to this prophet clothed in camel's hair. He preaches a message of repentance, baptizing in water those who receive the message. Now he says another will come and baptize, not in water but in the Holy Spirit.

What correlation did John intend between water baptism and the baptism in the Holy Spirit?

People on the banks of the Jordan River clearly understood "baptism" as "immersion." The message would have been obvious. Just as people were immersed in water, someone was coming who would "immerse" people in the Spirit of God. John was the "baptizer" in water, but Messiah himself would baptize in the Spirit.

In the Gospel of John's account of that day, John the Baptist announces Jesus' identity as the Lamb of God, the One who would baptize in the Spirit. John refers to the twofold ministry of Christ: first, as the One who removes sin from our lives; and second, as the One who fills us with His own Spirit.

For three years Jesus walked among people, healing the sick, performing miracles, teaching about His Father. Not until near the end did He talk about the Holy Spirit. Just before His Ascension He told the disciples they would receive power from on high (Luke 24:49). He ascended into heaven and left them anticipating the coming of the Spirit.

Receiving the Spirit's Power

In the Book of Acts, Luke says the following days were filled with prayer and study of the Scriptures. On the Day of Pentecost, a celebration day of the Jews, a supernatural phenomenon occurred which sounded like a violent wind from heaven. Unusual light, like tongues of fire, appeared on each of the disciples. Suddenly the praise of God welled in their hearts and every one of them began speaking in languages they had never learned. The disciples knew, without a doubt, this was the experience about which John the Baptist had spoken and for which Jesus had said to wait.

Luke reports two other occasions when the phenomenon of speaking in tongues occurred when people received the Holy Spirit. Gentiles received the Holy Spirit, prior to water baptism, at the household of Cornelius (Acts 10:44–46). Ephesian believers had a similar experience, after being baptized in water as a sign of their repentance (Acts 19:1–7).

In Acts 8, the Samaritans received the Holy Spirit but Luke does not mention speaking in tongues at this time.

What miraculous signs occurred in Samaria before the disciples came to pray for the Samaritans to receive the Holy Spirit?

When the apostles prayed for the Samaritans, something occurred that was different from the previous healings and miracles. The event was so unusual that Simon the Sorcerer offered money to be able to do as the apostles had done. Pentecostals contend that it must have been speaking in tongues, the same phenomenon mentioned in the other accounts.

In comparing these accounts, we discover no set pattern for receiving the Holy Spirit. Some received after a period of waiting, some received as soon as they heard the message. Some received after water baptism, some received before. However, the initial physical evidence of receiving the Holy Spirit is always speaking in tongues. The Holy Spirit still comes in fullness to those who are ready to receive Him.

Living by the Spirit's Leading

Receiving the Holy Spirit dynamically changed the lives of the believers in the Book of Acts as it does believers who receive Him today. The baptism in the Holy Spirit is only the beginning of a life of walking by the Spirit's leading.

What was the purpose of the Spirit's coming, according to Jesus?

The Holy Spirit was not only given to make the disciples feel good, although there was great joy among them after He came. Neither was He given only to set them apart from other people, although they did congregate in Christian community after the Spirit came. Jesus said the Spirit would come to impart power to be His witnesses.

Witnessing is what we *are*, not only what we *say* or *do*. Believers immersed in the Holy Spirit are to continue the ministry of Jesus on the earth, always pointing people to Him. They are not to be driven by self-effort or selfish gain. What they do should be the natural overflow of lives eternally changed by the coming of the Spirit.

How did believers witness for Jesus following the Day of Pentecost?

How is the Holy Spirit working in your life today?

Understand that every believer is a candidate for the infilling of the Holy Spirit, and for continuing to walk in His dynamic power. The only condition is faith to believe that Jesus will do as He promised.

One person who received the Holy Spirit on the Day of Pentecost was Jesus' own mother, Mary of Nazareth. She had been set apart by the Spirit to become the birth mother of Jesus more than thirty years before. She is mentioned a few times in the accounts of Jesus' ministry. Mary was a broken-hearted woman at the Cross. But Luke records she took her place with the disciples in the Upper Room, receiving the Holy Spirit when they did. Can you imagine her thoughts that day?

REFLECTING HIS IMAGE
Mary of Nazareth (Luke 1:26–56)

It's hard for people to remember that I was, am, and always will be a *real* woman. I never thought of myself as special. It wasn't the actual *appearance* of the angel so long ago that scared me. It was the *manner* of greeting. "Rejoice, highly favored one, the Lord is with you; blessed are you among women!"[1] What could I possibly have done to have found favor with God? I was just a nobody trying to exalt *somebody*—my Lord. And doesn't every human being owe that to the Creator?

The praise poem I recited to my cousin Elizabeth shortly after I learned that I was to be the mother of the promised Messiah, is a

---

[1]Luke 1:28, New King James Version.

tribute to God for the opportunity I had been given. Yes. I knew, loved, trusted, and exalted God in that moment. I still do.

I am not a magical figure. Through the years, I've had real problems, and failings. And despite the early evidence that Jesus was special, He honestly grew up so "normal" that even my vision sometimes became clouded where His identity was concerned. I had held Him as a baby, rocked Him, soothed Him, *and loved* Him. He was still my little child.

The day He missed the family caravan back to Nazareth, I was desperate. I demanded, "Young man, why have you done this to us? Your father and I have been half out of our minds looking for you."

He said, "Why were you looking for me? Didn't you know that I had to be here, dealing with the things of my Father?"[2]

As sensitive and responsive as I tried to be to Jesus, I was puzzled by His ministry and uncertain about what He was doing. After all, so many people charged Him with either being mad or in league with Satan that I found myself at times wanting to counsel Him, to calm Him, to urge Him to be less controversial.

Like so many others, I was simply waiting to see how God's purpose in Jesus would unfold. I never dreamed that purpose would find me holding His broken body at the foot of a cross. Again, I held Him, rocked Him, soothed Him, and loved Him. He was still my little child even though He grew up and set out on a course the direction of which neither I nor His brothers could fully understand.

Until now.

We—Jesus' disciples, His brothers, and the other women—left the mountain called Olives and returned to Jerusalem. It was a little over half a mile. In a pure act of obedience, we went to the Upper Room we had been using as a meeting place. I took my place with the others, unified in purpose and prayer. And my place was on my knees.

Suddenly, without a warning, I heard a sound like a strong wind, a gale. I couldn't tell where it came from as it filled all of the building. Then, like a wildfire, the Holy Spirit moved through those of us gathered and we began to speak in different languages as the Spirit encouraged us! Amazing!

---

[2]Luke 2:48,49, *The Message.*

Now I see. Now I understand. And what satisfies me is the only thing that will satisfy any person: a vital, daily relationship with God's Son, Jesus.

When I woke early this morning, I saw His face. I heard His voice. I remembered times spent together.

And I ask myself, *Have I done my best for Jesus?*

I wonder.

EMBRACING THE PENTECOSTAL PERSPECTIVE
What is the Holy Spirit teaching me?

Ever heard the phrase "wow factor"? This indefinable characteristic attracts our attention. In homes it is known as "curb appeal," in cars we speak of "great lines," and in clothing we look for "something special." What is it that makes Christians stand out from the crowd of religions, philosophies, and self-help gurus so prevalent today?

Always and forever, the answer is Jesus. And how do people see, hear, or encounter Jesus today? Through us! That's right. We are the billboard, the megaphone, the illustrated sermon. And the way that our lives—actions, beliefs, words, relationships, the whole package—have that irresistible "wow factor" is through the fullness of the Spirit.

Do you want to live in the fullness of the Spirit that comes through the baptism of the Spirit? Why or why not?

What holds you back from complete surrender to the Spirit?

Do you like good gifts? If so, why wait to ask for God's gift of the Spirit?

As invited in the opening page of this lesson, place yourself in the chaos of Jerusalem on the Day of Pentecost. Put yourself just an arm's length from Mary. Now imagine what it was like to hear a strange language flowing from her tongue. Though startled and uncertain, you are simultaneously fascinated. Instead of running in fear, you decide to stay and watch from a distance. The response amazes you. From Peter's message to people's hunger for Jesus, you are astounded by the strange mixture of audacity and love.

Paraphrase the Day of Pentecost events in your own setting (family reunion, daily workplace, retail center, neighborhood meeting, church service). What has prevented this from happening so far?

Think about the three thousand people who were saved on the Day of Pentecost and answer this question: What limits would you like to see God move above and beyond?

Receiving the baptism in the Spirit was never supposed to be anything more difficult than accepting a gift. Jesus told the disciples not to leave Jerusalem without it, and they obeyed. Complacency and cowardice ended. An unstoppable Church began. Today, we seem to complicate that dynamic simplicity—fixating on minutiae, creating faulty expectations. Jesus entrusted His Church with a mission impossible outside the power of the Holy Spirit. He said we needed the Holy Spirit, His Father's gift. What are we waiting for? Let's go—with the Holy Spirit!

If you ask for the Baptism and do not receive immediately with the initial evidence of speaking in tongues, will you continue to seek? Will you trust that this is God's will for you?

INVITING GOD TO CHANGE MY VIEW
What change is God asking me to make?

A friend just returned from a trip to Idaho, potato country, bringing a souvenir of chocolate covered potato chips. Each ridged chip was dunked in layers of delicious, creamy chocolate. Imagine the sheer delight of two choice snacks in combination.

Better than the transient joy of any food is the exciting truth that God chooses to work through us. Our weakness is covered by His strength; our shyness is cloaked in His boldness; our inability soaks up His supernatural ability; our deficits are filled with His fullness. Layer after layer of His glorious Spirit covers us, creating a combination that continues to baffle this world.

Are you living in the power of the Holy Spirit? Have you asked Jesus to be the Lord of your life? Are you staying full (Ephesians 5:18) of the Spirit as instructed? Do you need to use His power to witness more? Will you trust Him to keep His promises?

Prayer
Father, thank You for the gift of Your Holy Spirit. I understand that I could not come to Christ or receive salvation without Your Holy Spirit. Your generosity continues to amaze me. I trust that You know what is best for me. Sometimes I get ahead of You, and for that I ask

forgiveness. I do not want to live my life without You. I don't want to rush blindly into a future You have not ordained. Help me to wait on Your Spirit. Fill me afresh with Your Holy Spirit. Give me boldness as Your witness. Enable me to live daily in the power and joy of the Spirit's fullness. In Jesus' name, Amen.

JOURNALING

Take a few minutes to record your personal insights from the lesson.

Her Defining Character

CATCHING SIGHT
Introduction

A FAMILY, EXECUTING THEIR planned escape at midnight, dashes for the border; a man standing outside prison walls gulps fresh air; a woman, with every trace of the ravaging drug gone from her system, smiles wholeheartedly. The people in these vignettes share a commonality—they are free! With fresh anticipation, they can begin life anew.

Whether fleeing oppression, stepping out of prison, or breaking a habit, freedom means life. Nothing is as exhilarating as knowing the past is forgotten and new options await. People yearn to be free.

Christ died to set us free from sin and from a long list of laws and regulations. But we are not free to live as we want, because that would lead us back to selfish desire. Rather, we are now free to do what was impossible before—to live unselfishly! We can live this way as the Holy Spirit shapes our character into the likeness of Christ.

If we want the fruit of the Spirit, we must know Christ, love Him, and imitate Him. As a result, we will fulfill the intended purpose of the Law—to love God and our neighbors.

As you study the next four lessons, become aware of the two ways of living—for Christ and for self. You are free in Christ. Determine to live for Him by letting the Holy Spirit work in your life.

GETTING FOCUSED

Begin your study by considering the following:

With freedom comes responsibility. Name some examples of spiritual growth that have come into your life as you have matured in the Lord.

BIBLE READING

Galatians 5:19–25

Bold text indicates the verses emphasized in this lesson.

New International Version

19 **The acts of the sinful nature are obvious:** sexual immorality, impurity and debauchery; 20 **idolatry and witchcraft;** hatred, discord, jealousy, fits of rage, selfish ambition, dissensions, factions 21 and envy; drunkenness, orgies, and the like. I warn you, as I did before, that those who live like this will not inherit the kingdom of God.

22 **But the fruit of the Spirit is love, joy, peace,** patience, kindness, goodness, faithfulness, 23 gentleness and self-control. Against such things there is no law.
24 Those who belong to Christ Jesus have crucified the sinful nature with its passions and desires.
25 Since we live by the Spirit, let us keep in step with the Spirit.

New Living Translation

19 **When you follow the desires of your sinful nature, your lives will produce these evil results:** sexual immorality, impure thoughts, eagerness for lustful pleasure, 20 **idolatry, participation in demonic activities,** hostility, quarreling, jealousy, outbursts of anger, selfish ambition, divisions, the feeling that everyone is wrong except those in your own little group, 21 envy, drunkenness, wild parties, and other kinds of sin. Let me tell you again, as I have before, that anyone living that sort of life will not inherit the Kingdom of God.

22 **But when the Holy Spirit controls our lives, he will produce this kind of fruit in us: love, joy, peace,** patience, kindness, goodness, faithfulness, 23 gentleness, and self-control. Here there is no conflict with the law.

24 Those who belong to Christ Jesus have nailed the passions and

New Living Translation

desires of their sinful nature to his cross and crucified them there. 25 If we are living now by the Holy Spirit, let us follow the Holy Spirit's leading in every part of our lives.

GAINING BIBLICAL INSIGHT
Growing in God's likeness—love, joy, peace

*I*n Galatians, especially chapter 5, Paul paints a word picture of the striking contrast between the *acts of the sinful nature* and the *fruit of the Spirit.* This word picture shows how the Spirit affects every part of our being—spiritual, social, mental, and physical.

While these areas are intricately interrelated, viewing each separately helps us understand the potential depth of the Spirit's work in our lives. We will look at both the *acts of the sinful nature* and the *fruit of the Spirit* as each may be evident in the respective domains of our beings.

The Desire of the Human Spirit

Studies of human culture evidence that human beings have a spiritual dimension causing them to worship something beyond themselves. The source of this desire to worship is one focus of study for anthropologists and historians. Some say humankind has a psychological need for something to depend on, so people create a superhuman being in their thinking. This philosophy makes religion begin with man and makes God a product of man's imagination. While acknowledging man's need, this position does not explain the similarities of universal worship or exclude the existence of God.

Christians believe, along with the writer of Ecclesiastes, that God has put eternity in our hearts (Ecclesiastes 3:11). This position accepts a transcendent God who created human beings with a spiritual nature. The universal cultural evidence of worship of a divine being is consistent with this truth.

Misdirected Spiritual Relationships

Even a limited knowledge of history tells us humankind lost its way from what God intended at creation. The universal worship we observe usually takes forms contrary to what God commands in His Word. The First Commandment to Israel was that they should have no other gods before Jehovah. The second one restricted them from making graven images. The Scriptures record Israel's history of repeatedly departing from God's laws and falling into idolatry, followed by repentance and a return to the true worship of God.

Historically, how were idolatry and witchcraft defined?

Historically, idolatry was defined as "worship of pagan gods." However, idolatry may also be defined as misdirected worship or any worship that exalts created objects over God, the Creator. Worship contrary to God's Word may be categorized as idolatry. Witchcraft refers to magic or sorcery related to, or the outcome of, idolatry. In some cultures, the definition includes interaction with demonic spirits as acts of worship.

Why does Paul list idolatry and witchcraft as sins of the flesh?

Anything replacing God, as revealed in His Word, as the center of our worship may become an idol. When this happens, our carnal nature displaces our God-given desire to worship Him alone by focusing our adulation on other things. This misdirected worship is an act of the sinful nature.

The Holy Spirit Refining the Human Spirit

Paul told the Galatians they did not need to follow the pattern of their ancestors. He reminded them that they could be led by the Spirit, and so were not under the Law (verse 18). The work of the Holy Spirit within their lives would produce a different nature evidenced by certain characteristics, the first of which was *love*.

In studying the fruit of the Spirit, we note two dimensions of expression of that fruit. Some fruit will be seen in our relationship to God and some in our relationships with others. These qualities are the results of our growth in godliness.

In mentioning love first, Paul underscores what Jesus said would be the mark of Christian relationships (John 13:35). Jesus also summed up the commandments by saying there really are only two: to love God and to love our neighbors as ourselves. The Holy Spirit will help us become people who lavishly love both God and other people.

Love for God will be expressed first in our worship, displacing any tendency toward idolatry or curiosity about the magical arts of witchcraft and related cults. Because we love Him, nothing but God and His Word can be central to our lives. Our human spirit is in tune with the Spirit of God who directs us into the love of God. That love overflows into our relationships with people.

Love's companion is *joy*, which commentator Matthew Henry defines as "a constant delight in God." This joy, like our love relationship with God, also overflows into our interactions with people. Cheerfulness should be the usual tone of our exchange with others.

What difference do you see between joy and happiness?

Happiness is dependent upon circumstances. Joy abides in spite of circumstances because it is a work of the Holy Spirit in our lives. Joy comes from the Spirit within our hearts, not from a response to external circumstances.

The third work of the Holy Spirit on a human spirit is the restoration of *peace,* both with God and with other people. The peace the Spirit produces is an internal serenity, which comes from knowing God is in control of our life. It is an outflow of our love for Him, a settling of the joy of our relationship into the very depths of our being. Our soul is at rest because of our great trust in Him.

This kind of relationship with God affects our relationships with people. We do not want any human conflict to disrupt the deep peaceful relationship with our Heavenly Father. The love we have from Him produces joy and enables us to strive for peace in human relationships.

Sometimes situations require us to demonstrate love in tough circumstances. This was the case with Abigail in the Old Testament. When human conflict threatened to disrupt her entire life, she responded quickly. Note her gracious words as she confronts David. This manifestation of love for God and His people saved the situation and ultimately brought peace to Abigail's household.

REFLECTING HIS IMAGE
Abigail (1 Samuel 25)

In the midst of her own personal pain, Abigail knew that quick action was needed to undo what her husband had done. A wealthy sheep and goat herdsman, Nabal was also a prosperous property owner. Nabal made a serious mistake in judgment during sheepshearing in Carmel. *Other women are married to men like Nabal,* she reminded herself. *Mean, cruel, self-indulgent man. His foolish ways will be the death of us all!*

Just moments before, the frantic shepherd boy standing before Abigail had rushed in and started to speak. "Calm down! Collect your thoughts and tell me exactly what you heard," Abigail said.

The boy took a deep breath and began: "David, out in the back-country, heard Nabal was shearing sheep and sent messengers to salute our master. All David wanted was to have his men fed in return for protecting our herds. But our master tore into them with insults, saying, 'Who is this David anyway? Do you think I'm going to give good food and drink to men I've never laid eyes on? You must be crazy!' "

Abigail listened solemnly as the boy continued:

"My lady, these men of David's treated us kindly. They didn't take anything from us all the time we were in the fields. They formed a wall around us, protecting us day and night all the time we were tending the sheep.

"You've got to do something quickly! Four hundred of David's men are strapping on their swords. They'll kill us. All of us! Nobody can talk to Nabal. The master is impossible—a real brute!"

The shedding of more blood of God's people is unthinkable, Abigail thought to herself. "Tell no one of this," she said to the boy. "All will be known in due time."

Immediately assembling an array of foodstuffs, Abigail sent the gift ahead and set out to intercept David. She was determined to deal with the personal affront that had so angered him. *I barely remember what he looks like. What if he turns me away and refuses to listen to my request to think through the consequences of his reaction? What then? David himself knows that unnecessary bloodshed is wrong. Nabal might deserve death for insulting David, but to kill all the males in my household as David has vowed would cause innocent bloodshed.*

Her thoughts were interrupted as she spotted David coming down into the ravine ahead. *Help me not to panic, God,* she prayed. Coming closer and dismounting from the donkey which carried her, Abigail fell on her face before David and bowed down to the ground.

"My master, let me speak to you. Put the blame for these insults to your men on me. Nabal is a fool. I wasn't there to greet the young men you sent, but please, take this gift I have brought and give it to the young men who follow in your footsteps."

Her pulse raced as she continued.

"God is at work in you! When He completes the work He has started and makes you ruler of a united Israel, you won't have the guilt of a vengeful murder on your hands. Please, don't kill my family."

David's penetrating eyes softened as he looked at the brave and wise woman kneeling before him. She had reached into his soul to pull out his own better nature. Finally, he spoke. "Praise be to the Lord, the God of Israel, who has sent you today to meet me. May you be blessed for your good judgment and for keeping me from bloodshed."

Looking back on the events of the day before, Abigail was joyful that her family had been spared. And though she was married to a man whose name appropriately meant *fool,* she refused to accept his responses as her own. God had given her the ability to display love in hard circumstances. Even as Nabal lay suffering from heart failure after hearing the story she told him, and though she didn't know what would happen in her household, Abigail had peace. God had led her to act rightly, and she knew He would lead her in the days ahead.

EMBRACING THE PENTECOSTAL PERSPECTIVE
What is the Holy Spirit teaching me?

Character is often forged in defining moments. Sometimes these moments are obvious, as with Abigail's life-and-death action to intervene between her husband's foolishness and David's vengeance. Other times, the moments are simpler and less dramatic, but still profound, as most surely the reading of Paul's letter was to the Galatians. In life's pivotal moments, character is forged by our responses—a process both intensely personal and necessarily public.

We want to hear "Well done, good and faithful servant!"—words that require a life of Spirit-filled substance. We want to fulfill our call. Personally knowing God's love affects our ability to demonstrate that love.

Do you know—not just by way of fact, but in a way that brings assurance—that God truly loves you?

What do you do when you do not "feel" loving toward another person?

Have you discovered that the baptism in the Spirit enlarges your capacity to love others?

Many of us have tasted a really bad fat-free salad dressing. Not only are we surprised by the odd taste, but also the realization that "they missed by a mile" in imitating the original. We'd rather forget the calories and fat grams and take the real thing over the poor imitation every time. We should respond the same way to the abiding joy of life in the Spirit. Circumstantial happiness is a pitiful substitute for lasting joy. Lack of staying power makes the shortcomings of circumstantial happiness obvious.

When do you experience the greatest joy in your walk with the Lord?

Do you surrender your joy too easily in the face of trying circumstances? Why or why not?

How can you stop being an easy mark for the enemy when it comes to letting difficulty steal your joy?

Paul encouraged believers to enjoy the peace that rules in our hearts (Colossians 3:15). This peace acts as an umpire calling "safe!" in the midst of trials that would attempt to get us "out." For Abigail, this kind of peace enabled her to make and carry out a lifesaving plan. For you, it may be calm in the face of crisis, confidence under attack, or careful action under potentially inflammatory circumstances. Any way you look at it, it is a miracle of God's Spirit—one the world cannot help but notice.

How do you think peace feels in real life?

Describe one of your "anything but 'peace-full'" moments this week. Did you seek God's help immediately?

How can you access God's promised peace more quickly and constantly in your busy life?

INVITING GOD TO CHANGE MY VIEW
What change is God asking me to make?

Recent television crime dramas entertain a fascination with forensic studies. One program invites the viewer to "follow the evidence." Jesus taught that the world would know His followers by the fruit of their lives. Christians should so clearly evidence lives changed by the Spirit that others can follow them directly to the Source.

A friend once shared that she had to leave the lunchroom early at her job. She was tired of listening to another woman curse while wearing a "fruit of the Spirit" bracelet. Like this friend, most people— particularly those outside of Christ—are not impressed by Christian hardware. They want to see lives accessorized by the genuine articles of love, joy, and peace.

Are you living a life that invites others to "follow the evidence" to Christ? Would you like to begin your relationship with Christ and see this fruit develop in your life? Are you intentionally asking Jesus to produce the fruit of the Spirit in you? Are you struggling to love someone close to you right now? Would you like to access the joy God has for you in your current circumstances? Do you need peace to rule in your heart today?

Prayer
Heavenly Father, thank You for making new life possible through Your Son, Jesus. Nothing compares to this experience of being changed from the inside out. Continue to fill me with Your Holy Spirit and produce abundant fruit in my life. I want to overflow with love for You and this world that needs You. I want to exude a joy that supersedes circumstance and a peace that cannot be shaken. I stand upon Your promise to finish the good work that You have begun. In the precious name of Jesus, I ask these things. Amen.

JOURNALING
Take a few minutes to record your personal insights from the lesson.

Her Appropriate Responses

CATCHING SIGHT
Introduction

LOOK AROUND YOU and find five things that have blue in them. With a "blue" mindset, you'll find that blue "jumps out" at you: a blue book on the table, a blue pillow on the couch, blue in the painting on the wall, and so on. You've also probably noticed that after you buy a new car, you see that make and model of car repeatedly. That's because people find what they are looking for—what they have a mindset for.

The virtues from Galatians define Christlikeness and summarize the character mindset God wants every Christian to develop. In nine words we describe as *the fruit of the Spirit,* God provides us with His standard of true spirituality. Contrary to how we usually judge, this standard focuses on what we are, not on what we do. The fruit of the Spirit is a natural outgrowth of a life that is lived pleasing the Lord. When we have the fruit of the Spirit in our lives, we will respond to stressful circumstances in an appropriate manner.

If we are going to display the fruit of the Spirit in our lives daily, we must develop our sensitivity to the quiet voice of the Holy Spirit. At times in our lives, God may seem strangely absent, but the problem is not that God has disappeared. The problem may be that we simply lack a "God" mindset.

GETTING FOCUSED
Begin your study by considering the following:

Have you ever prayed for patience? Did God answer your prayer? If so, in what way?

BIBLE READING
Galatians 5:19–25

Bold text indicates the verses emphasized in this lesson.

New International Version

19 **The acts of the sinful nature are obvious:** sexual immorality, impurity and debauchery; 20 idolatry and witchcraft; hatred, **discord, jealousy,** fits of rage, **selfish ambition, dissensions, factions** 21 **and envy;** drunkenness, orgies, and the like. I warn you, as I did before, that those who live like this will not inherit the kingdom of God.

22 **But the fruit of the Spirit is** love, joy, peace, **patience, kindness, goodness,** faithfulness, 23 gentleness and self-control. Against such things there is no law. 24 Those who belong to Christ Jesus have crucified the sinful nature with its passions and desires. 25 Since we live by the Spirit, let us keep in step with the Spirit.

New Living Translation

19 **When you follow the desires of your sinful nature, your lives will produce these evil results:** sexual immorality, impure thoughts, eagerness for lustful pleasure, 20 idolatry, participation in demonic activities, hostility, **quarreling, jealousy,** outbursts of anger, **selfish ambition, divisions, the feeling that everyone is wrong except those in your own little group,** 21 envy, drunkenness, wild parties, and other kinds of sin. Let me tell you again, as I have before, that anyone living that sort of life will not inherit the Kingdom of God.

22 **But when the Holy Spirit controls our lives, he will produce this kind of fruit in us:** love, joy, peace, **patience, kindness, goodness,** faithfulness, 23 gentleness, and self-control. Here there is no conflict with the law.

24 Those who belong to Christ Jesus have nailed the passions and desires of their sinful nature to his

New Living Translation

cross and crucified them there. 25 If
we are living now by the Holy
Spirit, let us follow the Holy Spirit's
leading in every part of our lives.

GAINING BIBLICAL INSIGHT
Learning to relate like Jesus—patience, goodness, kindness

Not good!" God said. This was the only time He described anything
in His creation that way. Everything else met His divine approval.
And what was "not good"? A solitary man. "Man should not be
alone," God said, so He created a woman as a companion for the
man. Since that moment in the Garden, people have lived in social
groups—first in families, then in communities, followed by states
and nations.

In today's social structure, we may find ourselves in many circles
of relationships which form for different reasons. Ideally, relationships are smooth when people come together in groups. Realistically,
too often that is not so. Personality conflicts fracture families and
make work environments difficult. Discord between opposing ideas
polarizes communities, states, and nations. Peace disappears from our
social structure as people respond to conflict and discord in self-
serving ways.

One work of the Holy Spirit in the lives of Christians is to produce
fruit that will enable us to live together in peace. The principles for
relating to one another in mutually beneficial ways apply in all circles of relationship throughout our social structure.

Problems in Relationships

In Galatians 5, Paul refers to several sins of the flesh which inter-fere with healthy relationships. *Discord,* or open conflict in relation-ships, is usually evidence of deeper personality problems. As we look at the list of sins of the flesh, we note the common characteristic of relational problems is a general feeling of ill will which manifests itself in different ways.

Jealousy and *envy* are two related emotions which can produce strife. **How do you differentiate between jealousy and envy?**

Jealousy and envy both have their roots in the feeling that some-one else has something desirable which we do not have. We can be jealous of another's looks, talents, skills, or anything that seems to promote that person ahead of us, getting them more admiration from others, or placing them in a more advantageous position. From this root, we develop strong feelings against that person, accompa-nied by the tendency to find fault with anything they do. The spirit of rivalry, which may result, produces discord or strife.

Envy is usually directed to the possessions themselves rather than the person. However, if left unchecked, envy can grow into malicious actions toward the person. For example, the Bible tells us that Jesus was betrayed because of envy (Matthew 27:18). Envy, like jealousy, is often found as the cause of strife in many circles of relationships.

Strife may come also because of differing opinions. In this list, Paul refers to *dissensions* and *factions* which result from conflicting views about issues or procedures. First, people are dissentious with each other, unable to resolve differences. Then people form factions as they take sides over issues.

Paul mentions another act of the flesh in this list, however, that contributes to all the above problems. *Selfish ambition* may be the cause of jealousy and envy. It may contribute to dissension and the formulation of factions within groups. One of the major hindrances in human relationships in any setting—the home, school, church, or community—exists when someone self-centeredly insists on having her own way. Self-promoting is an odious act of sinful flesh which should have no place in the life of a Christian.

Building Relationships with the Help of the Spirit

One of the purposes of the coming of the Holy Spirit is to help us in relationships with each other. Having experienced the love of God at work in our lives, which has brought joy and peace to our hearts, we are ready to show that love to others through patience, goodness, and kindness. This is not something we do within ourselves, but it is the working of the Holy Spirit in our lives.

In the great love chapter, 1 Corinthians 13, patience is the first definition of love. It is closely followed by kindness and several qualities which demonstrate goodness. These three—patience, kindness, and goodness—work together as a function of God's grace in our hearts.

Patience refers to that attribute of character which enables us to keep our own spirit under control in spite of the frustrations or tedium of life. It is an internal work within our own spirit. It enables us to refrain from inappropriate responses in situations that might otherwise be stressful or cause strife.

Kindness is the outflow of patience and refers to our treatment of other people. It is the manifestation of a benevolent spirit in a situation which does not warrant it. By demonstrating kindness, we reflect the kindness of God toward us.

What relationship do you see between patience and kindness?

Often, it is impatience that causes us to be unkind. We feel inner frustration because of circumstances or people's actions which cause us to be impatient with them. We express that impatience in unkind words and deeds.

What enables us to be patient and kind is the goodness the Spirit produces within us. The word *goodness* here is used most often to describe the essential goodness of God. The implication is that the very nature of God is formed in us by the working of the Holy Spirit. As we learn to yield to Him, rather than giving way to the natural tendencies of the flesh, God produces the fruit of the Spirit in our lives.

Priscilla, a New Testament businesswoman, demonstrated the essential goodness of God as she and her husband partnered with Paul in the ministry. Together, they showed kindness to the young minister, Apollos, who needed further teaching in the things of the Lord. Patiently in their home, away from public view, they explained the way of the Lord more adequately. Their goodness, kindness, and patience paid off as the maturing Apollos preached to the new Ephesian Christians and God responded by pouring His Spirit on them. Let's glance at what Priscilla's journal might have looked like.

REFLECTING HIS IMAGE
Priscilla (Acts 18:18–26)

Journal Entry
Thursday

Yesterday we landed in Ephesus where Aquila and I got off the boat and decided to stay. Our dear friend and fellow worker Paul left the ship briefly to go to the meeting place and preach to the Jews. They wanted him to stay longer, but he said he couldn't. But after saying good-bye, he promised, "I'll be back, God willing."[1]

---

[1]Acts 18:19–21, *The Message.*

Journal Entry
Monday

We learned that after Paul left Ephesus he sailed to Caesarea. After greeting the assembly of Christians there, he went on to Antioch, completing his journey. Hosting a house-church, supporting Paul's ministry, and teaching and instructing from city to city continue to be great joys in our lives and our marriage. It is not an easy life, but the Holy Spirit brings us patience.

I was thinking earlier today, what an amazing privilege for us to have access to God through Christ!

Journal Entry
Wednesday

A man named Apollos came to Ephesus today. He spoke in the synagogue. He was a terrific speaker, eloquent and powerful in his preaching of the Scriptures. He was accurate in everything he taught about Jesus up to a point, but he only went as far as the baptism of John.[2] Aquila and I were silent, not wanting to disrupt in any way, which took a great deal of patience. We did not want to bring discord among the believers, and we wanted to show kindness to Apollos. So later we took him aside and told him how God has given His Spirit to His people. Apollos's response to correction was in a beautiful, Christlike manner, so appropriate for a sincere believer.

Journal Entry
Friday

Aquila looks especially tired tonight. How grateful I am that he is my life partner! He teaches me what it is to be kind. I am learning day by day that true partnership is achieved as we continue to live together as one in *all* things. Neither of us is the leader, neither is the follower. We share in common our life and ministry here on earth. The Holy Spirit has been and is our Helper, both in our personal lives and ministry. Help me, Lord, to remain true to my commitments and my responses, not only to Your people but to my husband as well.

[2] Acts 18:24,25, *The Message.*

EMBRACING THE PENTECOSTAL PERSPECTIVE
What is the Holy Spirit teaching me?

Priscilla's journal reads like a fairy tale—almost too good to be true. She manages to react with courage and goodwill in an unfamiliar setting, gratitude in the midst of hard work, consideration when condescension might seem justified, and genuine desire for growth while weary from the present demands. How did she do it?

The good life Priscilla experienced had little to do with her circumstances. Her story inspires real hope because it illustrates perfectly the power of the Holy Spirit to change us. God works transformation through the Spirit, enabling us to grow beyond the bad habits of the old life. A chief offender in the brigade of bad habits is impatience. God requires patience with people, circumstances, and even ourselves.

How has your patience been tested lately? Did you pass the test?

Both Jesus and James instructed believers that they "don't have, because they don't ask" and that we need to pray believing (Luke 11:9; James 4:2,3). **Have you prayed, with faith, for patience in your mind and spirit?**

Patience is half the battle in our relationships. It would not be nearly so hard to exhibit kindness to others—deserving or not—if we hadn't already allowed frustration to call the shots with our words or actions.

Sitting in a drive-through lane recently for just slightly less than eternity, a believer erupted with exasperation after finally advancing to the window. The bewildered clerk doubled her small order to make up for the inconvenience. Hindsight showed the woman how an inappropriate response on her part destroyed any chance she had at being the extender, rather than recipient, of kindness.

If you accept the premise that the world definitely suffers from a kindness drought, explain how you could demonstrate kindness in your everyday travels.

Do you believe kindness is conditional upon the other person's actions or upon your own responsiveness to the Spirit? Is that normally how you react?

Following Jesus is a challenge. Conventional means—personal strength, trying harder, giving it your best—just won't deliver the changed life promised in His Word. Radical change grows out of God's radical goodness. He does the right things in the right way, because He is righteous and good. We can do the same, but only with intense dependence on the Holy Spirit.

In the context of your own life, how can you demonstrate more goodness?

What bad habits would you like to see replaced by goodness?

How would this world respond to inexplicable acts of goodness?

INVITING GOD TO CHANGE MY VIEW
What change is God asking me to make?

Those of us who have taught a young child to use new motor skills, like riding a bike or threading a needle, shooting a basket or holding a pencil, realize that, at some point, the child reaches the limits of patience. Throwing the object down, the child is convinced the task is impossible. We may even hear the excuses, "I can't do this. It's too hard. I'm not strong enough (or smart, fast, big enough)." We chuckle, knowing the child is just one or two more attempts from catching on to the new skill.

As believers, we need to remember to apply the same learning curve principles to our spiritual formation. Rather than excusing ourselves as not cut out for patience, or blaming our personalities, parents, or present emotional states for our lack of love or kindness, we need to pray for more of God's Spirit.

Your prayer might take one of these forms: "Lord, I need patience with (fill in the blank). I do believe you can develop patience in my life. Grant me the mindset of God. Help me to become a responder according to the pattern of Christ. Jesus, be my Lord. I want to act like You, from the inside out. Test me, prove me."

Prayer

Father, thank You for Your patience with me. Without Your daily good-ness and kindness—everything from the beauty of the sunrise to the reassuring reminders of Your grace throughout the day—I could not make it. I really do want to be a reflection of You. Help me to start by being more responsive to the gentle leading of Your Spirit. Stop me from barging through life with my obnoxious habits. Forgive me for excusing myself with lame jokes. I would so much rather respond from a changed heart. Amen.

JOURNALING

Take a few minutes to record your personal insights from the lesson.

Her Contagious Attitude

CATCHING SIGHT
Introduction

*H*AVE YOU EVER tried to keep an attractive fruit basket on your kitchen table for more than a few days? Soon, this thing of beauty becomes a dwelling for fruit flies and fuzzy gray mold. Fruit is meant to be consumed. Likewise, the Spirit's fruit must not be tucked away in your heart, but should be fed to sad, love-starved, stressed-out people. You must not bear fruit to hoard it selfishly.

Our attitudes color our personalities. We cannot always choose what happens to us, but we can choose our attitudes toward each situation. The secret is filling our minds with thoughts that are true, pure, and lovely—thoughts that dwell on God's goodness. Look at your attitude and examine what you allow to enter your mind and what you choose to dwell on. Don't allow others' values and actions to dictate your attitude and behavior.

When we stand before Jesus, will He only mark our attendance? Or will He be able to say, "Well done, My good and faithful servant"?

GETTING FOCUSED
Begin your study by considering the following:

In what ways can our attitudes become carbon copies of the world's? Name some ways that our attitudes can reflect the humility and self-sacrifice of Jesus.

BIBLE READING
Galatians 5:19–25

Bold text indicates the verses emphasized in this lesson.

New International Version

19 **The acts of the sinful nature are obvious:** sexual immorality, impurity and debauchery; 20 idolatry and witchcraft; **hatred, discord, jealousy, fits of rage, selfish ambition, dissensions, factions** 21 **and envy;** drunkenness, orgies, and the like. I warn you, as I did before, that those who live like this will not inherit the kingdom of God.

22 **But the fruit of the Spirit is** love, joy, peace, patience, kindness, goodness, **faithfulness,** 23 **gentleness** and self-control. Against such things there is no law. 24 Those who belong to Christ Jesus have crucified the sinful nature with its passions and desires. 25 Since we live by the Spirit, let us keep in step with the Spirit.

New Living Translation

19 **When you follow the desires of your sinful nature, your lives will produce these evil results:** sexual immorality, impure thoughts, eagerness for lustful pleasure, 20 idolatry, participation in demonic activities, **hostility, quarreling, jealousy, outbursts of anger, selfish ambition, divisions, the feeling that everyone is wrong except those in your own little group,** 21 **envy,** drunkenness, wild parties, and other kinds of sin. Let me tell you again, as I have before, that anyone living that sort of life will not inherit the Kingdom of God.

22 **But when the Holy Spirit controls our lives, he will produce this kind of fruit in us:** love, joy, peace, patience, kindness, goodness, **faithfulness,** 23 **gentleness,** and self-control. Here there is no conflict with the law.

24 Those who belong to Christ Jesus have nailed the passions and

New Living Translation

desires of their sinful nature to his cross and crucified them there. 25 If we are living now by the Holy Spirit, let us follow the Holy Spirit's leading in every part of our lives.

GAINING BIBLICAL INSIGHT

Choosing my thoughts with care—faithfulness, gentleness

The Importance of Mindset

*B*efore the invention of the steamboat, sailing was the major means of water transportation. Early European ships had square sails, designed to sail only in favorable winds. Triangular sails became popular later because they could be turned to catch winds from different directions, increasing the possibilities for sailing. Later, sails were designed that caused the ship to fly against the wind.

With this knowledge, poet Ella Wheeler Wilcox (1850–1919) wrote these lines which have almost become legendary:

One ship drives east and other drives west
With the self-same winds that blow;
'Tis the set of the sails
And not the gales that tells them the way to go.[1]

With these brief lines, Wilcox illustrates the importance of mental attitude. Like a sailboat, our lives are affected not so much by circumstances as by the way we approach them. In Paul's writings to the Galatians, we can see the importance of mental attitude as it affects our emotions and actions.

---

[1]Ella Wheeler Wilcox, *The Winds of Fate*, www.ellawheelerwilcox.org (accessed on 10/28/04).

The Effect of Negative Mental Expressions

While the discussion of negative attitude could include many expressions, the specific area mentioned in Galatians is *hatred* with its *fits of rage*. Hatred begins in the mind, continues with the emotions, and finally involves the will as it expresses itself in angry fits of rage. In the Sermon on the Mount, Jesus emphasizes the importance of controlling anger before it leads to disastrous consequences (Matthew 5:21,22).

How is hatred related to the acts of the sinful nature which we have previously studied?

In looking at hatred, we can see how closely all the acts of the sinful nature are related. Hatred may be spawned by jealousy or envy. It may be the cause of dissension or factions. A root cause of hatred may be frustrated selfish ambition.

What is the difference between hating and disliking someone?

All of us are different. Our emotions can range from liking someone to indifference to hatred. We will not like everyone we meet as we may not have commonalities which promote friendship. Hatred is an intensity of feeling that may begin with disliking someone, but as negative thoughts seethe within the mind, disliking becomes loathing, detesting, or abhorring. Hatred fosters bitterness that leads to anger, which may express itself in fits of rage.

Is it ever appropriate for a Christian to become angry?

It is important to note here the difference between anger as an emotion and the expression of anger in fits of rage. All of us feel varying degrees of anger at different times in our lives. We have petty irritations, such as having to wait too long in a line or being cut off in traffic. We are annoyed by noisy neighbors and frustrated with the demands of bureaucracy. These are normal responses to minor injustices.

In this passage, Paul is concerned with uncontrolled outbursts of anger that result from sinful human nature. The problem is not anger itself, but how we deal with this emotion and accompanying mindset. Fits of rage are always inappropriate for Christians.

So, how do Christians deal with anger and intense feelings of bitterness or hatred toward other people? We call upon the Holy Spirit to produce a Christlike spirit in us, which will change our attitude.

The Influence of the Holy Spirit on My Attitude

The next two fruit of the Spirit to be discussed are *faithfulness* and *gentleness*. These character traits are in contrast to *hatred* and *fits of rage,* which are acts of the sinful nature.

Faithfulness here refers to authenticity or consistency between belief and practice. It includes honesty and integrity in relationships with others, as well as trustworthiness and dependability. A faithful woman will not explode into fits of rage, because she demonstrates stability in her personality, an evenness produced by the presence of the Holy Spirit and His working in her life.

Likewise, a faithful woman cannot harbor hatred in her heart, because she professes to have the love, joy, and peace of God dwelling there. Such behavior would be inconsistent with her belief in the love of God. If she experiences circumstances which might cause her to be bitter or to hate someone, she has a choice to make.

She can respond from her old nature and let hatred and bitterness reside in her heart, or she can ask the Holy Spirit to remove these negative emotions from her. The Spirit will do a work in her heart so she can be described as a faithful woman—someone whose practice matches her belief. This is authentic Christianity.

Gentleness includes the related graces of meekness and humility. By maintaining a spirit of meekness, we have the ability to overcome passions aroused by anger and resentment which produce hatred. Love is "not easily angered, it keeps no record of wrongs," Paul wrote in 1 Corinthians 13:5. This is another way of describing the meek and gentle person who maintains the right attitude when circumstances are wrong.

The interesting thing about attitude is that it is contagious, affecting the people with whom we come in contact. One angry person in a group of people can change the climate of conversation. Hatred in someone's heart will permeate her conversation like garlic permeates the food around it.

Thankfully, a gentle person's spirit can also be contagious. "A gentle answer turns away wrath, but a harsh word stirs up anger" (Proverbs 15:1). The best antidotes for hatred and anger are the gentleness and faithfulness of authentic Christians.

Sadly, however, people who have been used of the Lord can let jealousy be expressed in anger. Not only will they be affected by their unfaithful actions, but others will be hurt also. Such was the case with Miriam, sister of Moses, whose jealousy was punished by leprosy. Though she was mercifully healed by the Lord, the whole nation of Israel was halted in its progress to Canaan. Let's hear her story.

REFLECTING HIS IMAGE
Miriam (Exodus 2:1–10; 15:20,21; Numbers 12:1–15; Deuteronomy 24:9)

Miriam held her breath as she applied soothing oil to the leprous sores on her legs and arms. Pain gripped her.

The anger of God had blazed out against her for talking against her brother Moses behind his back. The result: an infectious skin disease and seven days of isolation. And now, displeased with her own negative attitude, she sat alone, excluded from her Israelite family. God had exposed her sinful heart.

Miriam's limbs ached from the damp and cold of her surroundings. *How did I come to this place, God? I wonder. I was an obedient daughter, a protective big sister, a prophet, and a worship leader.* Yet as she pondered in her heart, she knew. Miriam was not above human frailty. Pride and selfish ambition had gotten in her way.

Five days earlier, God had spoken to her, Moses, and Aaron in a pillar of cloud as He stood at the entrance to the Tent of Meeting.

"Listen carefully to what I'm telling you.
    If there is a prophet of GOD among you,
I make myself known to him in visions,
    I speak to him in dreams.
But I don't do it that way with my servant Moses;
    he has the run of my entire house;
I speak to him intimately, in person,
    in plain talk without riddles:
    He ponders the very form of GOD.
So why did you show no reverence or respect
    in speaking against my servant, against
    Moses?"[1]

Why indeed? Miriam thought. She was the leader of the women who led Israel in worship after the deliverance at the Red Sea and called for the community to "sing to the LORD" in a spontaneous and joyous moment of pure worship (Exodus 15:21). God used her as a prophet in a position of leadership. She knew she had an extra responsibility to honor God as well as her leader, Moses.

Miriam broke down and sobbed. *How often have I held on to my sin, letting it grow until it affected my relationships with others and with You, O God? I confess that I was bitter and angry with You when You told me what I had done. I came to believe I was justified in my jealousy and thoughtlessness and self-importance. Forgive me for leading Aaron into my own negative thoughts. Aaron and I have important*

[1]Numbers 12:6–8, *The Message*, emphasis added.

ministries of our own, but You have chosen Moses as our leader. I know that now. O Lord, I will rejoice in the gifts You have given me, fulfilled in serving where I am. Have mercy on me!

On other days, Miriam would examine her motives and thoughts toward her family and community. But now she stood tall under God's scrutiny.

If God were to expose our sinful hearts as He did with Miriam, who would be left with flawless skin?

EMBRACING THE PENTECOSTAL PERSPECTIVE
What is the Holy Spirit teaching me?

"I could just kick myself!" Had Miriam been familiar with our contemporary vernacular, surely she would have used this expression. Similar echoes would have been heard from Mary mother of Jesus after hearing her twelve-year-old divine Son's answer to her demanding question; from Peter in the shockwave of "Get behind me, Satan"; from James and John when they suggested a dose of heavenly fire for some irritating bystanders; and from Martha after erupting with self-righteous indignation at her Guest of honor.

What do these biblical personalities have in common? All of these occasions were marked by varying degrees of seriousness—nothing life-threatening—followed by significant growth. We share their experiences, the unbridled moments of bad attitudes and headstrong insistence. These inevitably lead us outside Christlike behavior and beyond the Spirit's transforming work. Kicking ourselves will not accomplish anything; seeking spiritual growth will work miracles in our lives. We can join Miriam, Mary, Peter, James, John, and Martha in the experience of restoration and productive behavior.

What is your more problematic "kick yourself" condition— an unbridled tongue or impulsive actions?

Is your attitude dependent on the current circumstances?

How have you seen the contagious nature of an attitude—either positive or negative?

Disconnecting what we believe and how we act has implications beyond the obvious hypocritical witness. Failure to bring our actions into alignment with our faith causes a short circuit in that faith! It is very difficult to believe for the miraculous when we do not see any change in the mundane. In contrast, recognizing growth in the fruit of the Spirit encourages our faith for greater things.

Conduct a faithfulness inventory of your life. What components would you inspect for proof of faithfulness?

Miriam's hurdle to consistent faithfulness was pride. What is yours?

Some suggest counting to ten before responding to an antagonistic situation (anything from a three-year-old's maddening string of questions to the accusations of an enraged customer). While delay tactics can sometimes derail emotions, often they simply serve to escalate them. A better response might be to engage in a purposeful act of prayer. Ask the Lord to calm your spirit and fill you with His strength. Then you can respond with a gentleness that infuses the situation with a different spirit.

Explain how gentleness requires great strength, as opposed to having a doormat attitude.

In what relationships do you need to demonstrate more gentleness? How would your personal spiritual growth in gentleness affect that relationship?

INVITING GOD TO CHANGE MY VIEW
What change is God asking me to make?

The importance of faithfulness and gentleness was made vividly clear at a community airport. The landing strip stood atop a small mountain, with drop-offs at either end. The airport manager shared stories of disastrous landings at each end. One plane landed long and ran off the runway, severely damaging the plane, but the pilot walked away from the crash. At the opposite end, a pilot failed to remove the control lock on the plane's steering, which resulted in a crash with multiple fatalities.

These two cases mirror our responses to the guidance of the Holy Spirit. When we go beyond the bounds of behavior reflecting God's faithfulness—either by poor choices or carelessness—we cause embarrassment to ourselves and damage to others. If we fail to reside in a place of gentleness—choosing to maintain control of our own lives, rather than submitting to the strength of the Spirit—disaster results. Between the two extremes exists an exhilarating life, guided by the Spirit, controlled by grace, and capable of moving others to worthwhile destinations.

Do you need an attitude adjustment of the Spirit kind? Do you overestimate your own opinions and worth and leave others disappointed? Have you kept the steering of your life under your own control? Do you need to surrender your life, your disaster, your weakness to Jesus? Will you ask for the fruit of faithfulness and gentleness today?

Prayer

Dear Lord, I confess my need for more of Your Spirit. Just when I think I have my act together, I am reminded that life is not supposed to be an act. I am neither the author nor finisher of my faith, and I desperately need You to bring change in me. Help me to think like You do, to see others as You do. Give me a mouth that is slow to speak words of anger or negativity, and enable me to boldly express encouragement. Replace my impulsive words and actions with gentle, strong, grace-filled ones. For Jesus' sake, Amen.

JOURNALING

Take a few minutes to record your personal insights from the lesson.

Her Tenacious Integrity

CATCHING SIGHT
Introduction

*D*O YOU ENJOY shopping for a new car? When looking at cars, we usually make a list of features we need and features that are optional. We might need fuel efficiency, air conditioning, and room for five adults. But it's optional that the car have a moon roof, leather bucket seats, and a spoiler. It might be mandatory that the car have a comfortable ride and side air bags, but a DVD player and a deluxe CD package are optional.

Mistaking our needs for our wants is easy. We mistake an urgent need for an expendable want. Such is the case with integrity. Many people act as if integrity is optional for a Christian's life. Scripture tells us that it is mandatory.

Adam and Eve mistook God's mandatory command for an optional choice. "Am I my brother's keeper?" asked Cain, after killing Abel. Moses never entered the Promised Land because he learned too late that small matters of integrity were mandatory. Samson had supernatural strength, but he died in captivity because of his problem with lust.

Integrity is telling the truth and living the truth. It comes from the same root word as *integration*. When we integrate truth into our lives, we have integrity. Build the type of integrity you can stake your life on. Accept the fact that integrity is not optional, like leather bucket seats, but mandatory, like wheels!

GETTING FOCUSED
Begin your study by considering the following:

How do you feel when someone behaves as if integrity is only an accessory?

BIBLE READING
Galatians 5:19–25

Bold text indicates the verses emphasized in this lesson.

New International Version

19 **The acts of the sinful nature are obvious: sexual immorality, impurity and debauchery;** 20 idolatry and witchcraft; hatred, discord, jealousy, fits of rage, selfish ambition, dissensions, factions 21 and envy; **drunkenness, orgies, and the like.** I warn you, as I did before, that those who live like this will not inherit the kingdom of God.

22 **But the fruit of the Spirit is** love, joy, peace, patience, kindness, goodness, faithfulness, 23 gentleness and **self-control.** Against such things there is no law. 24 Those who belong to Christ Jesus have crucified the sinful nature with its passions and desires. 25 Since we live by the Spirit, let us keep in step with the Spirit.

New Living Translation

19 **When you follow the desires of your sinful nature, your lives will produce these evil results: sexual immorality, impure thoughts, eagerness for lustful pleasure,** 20 idolatry, participation in demonic activities, hostility, quarreling, jealousy, outbursts of anger, selfish ambition, divisions, the feeling that everyone is wrong except those in your own little group, 21 envy, **drunkenness, wild parties, and other kinds of sin.** Let me tell you again, as I have before, that anyone living that sort of life will not inherit the Kingdom of God.

22 **But when the Holy Spirit controls our lives, he will produce this kind of fruit in us:** love, joy, peace, patience, kindness, goodness, faithfulness, 23 gentleness, and **self-control.** Here there is no conflict with the law.

24 Those who belong to Christ

New Living Translation

Jesus have nailed the passions and desires of their sinful nature to his cross and crucified them there. 25 If we are living now by the Holy Spirit, let us follow the Holy Spirit's leading in every part of our lives.

GAINING BIBLICAL INSIGHT
Keeping my thoughts pure before God—self-control

Wholeness in the Christian Life

*I*f you talk the talk, then walk the walk" is a phrase we commonly hear, emphasizing the necessity for Christians to live by their beliefs. This is the same appeal Paul makes at the conclusion of this passage on the life of the Spirit: "Since we live by the Spirit, let us keep in step with the Spirit" (Galatians 5:25).

His plea is for integrity in the Christian life, a unity between what we say we believe and how we live. The Holy Spirit helps us by producing His fruit in our lives. In listing the various works of the Spirit, Paul concludes with *self-control,* which is needed in every part of our lives—spiritual, mental, and physical. In this lesson, we look at how self-control is needed specifically in the physical dimension, if we are to have lives of integrity.

Violations in the Physical Realm

A high standard of sexual purity is maintained throughout Scripture. Adultery was forbidden by the Old Testament Law (Exodus 20:14). Early Church elders did not ask Gentile believers to keep the entire Law, but requested that they maintain sexual purity (Acts 15:20). Jesus taught that not only were *acts* of sexual promiscuity wrong, but also *the thoughts and emotions behind those acts*—even if the act was not actually committed (Matthew 5:27,28).

In Paul's list of acts of the sinful nature, he elaborates on *sexual immorality* by adding *impurity,* which refers to thoughts as well as actions. He goes one step further and adds *debauchery,* which refers to the moral attitude of shamelessness about these illicit sexual indulgences.

Why do you think the Bible places such preeminence on sexual purity?

One consideration may be the high priority God places on human life. He protected the act of giving life through appropriate sexual union by condemning adultery. Likewise, He recognized the right to a natural death by condemning murder. The implication is that life is sacred, including its beginning in the context of sacred marriage.

Consideration must also be given to God's view of what happens in sexual union: The man and woman become one flesh (Genesis 2:24; Ephesians 5:31). This mystical union is violated by adultery and fornication.

A further consideration must be an understanding of God's view of the human body. While some philosophies view the body as evil, the Christian knows the body is the temple of God's Spirit. Christians seek to honor God by avoiding sexual immorality as a sin against the body (1 Corinthians 6:18–20).

Along with sexual immorality, Paul discusses other sins of excess: *drunkenness, orgies, and the like.* This is not an exhaustive list, but some examples of sins of intemperance. He refers not only to personal involvement with excessive drinking, but also to shameful orgies involving groups of inebriated people. Too often, drunkenness leads to the other sins of the flesh, which Paul condemns.

A very serious indictment follows this list of the acts of the sinful nature. Those who do these things, Paul says, "will not inherit the kingdom of God." This reference includes the entire list, not just sexual immorality and drunkenness, which we may consider more abhorrent.

Maintaining Physical Purity with the Help of the Spirit

As we ponder Paul's statement, we might ask ourselves, "What chance do we have of making it? Don't we all lapse into the sins of the flesh sometimes?" We find our answer as we read on. Yes, we all have the potential of yielding to our sinful natures, but the Holy Spirit is given to help us live victorious lives as He works in us.

For example, when it comes to maintaining physical and mental purity, we can succeed with the help of the Holy Spirit. However, we must cooperate with Him by doing all we can to avoid temptation in these areas.

What effect will the desire to maintain physical purity have on our daily lives? Will it affect what we read? Our conversation? Our entertainment?

We cannot expect the Holy Spirit to keep our minds pure when we feed on impure conversations, reading material, television programs, videos, or movies. When we exercise our will to make a choice for purity by changing off-color conversations, getting rid of offensive literature, and avoiding objectionable entertainment, the Holy Spirit gives us strength to maintain our stand. *Self-control* is a fruit of His presence.

In this series of lessons, we have discussed eight character traits the Holy Spirit desires to produce within us. The last one—self-control—affects all the others. For example, self-control helps us be patient, kind, and gentle. The other traits involve our spirits, emotions, and minds. But this one involves our will and requires our cooperation with the Holy Spirit. He wants to help us live disciplined lives, but we must let Him work in us. He will produce that tenacious integrity we desire in our lives. Our behavior will match our belief.

Paul makes an interesting concluding statement: "Against such things there is no law." The Old Testament Law forbade the sins of the flesh Paul listed, but it made no difference. People continued in their sins, even though they knew they were wrong. But Paul explains there is no law against the working of the Spirit. These qualities cannot be acquired by keeping the Law, nor are they forbidden by the Law. They are a work of the Holy Spirit. The fruit of the Spirit grow from love, which is the fulfillment of the Law. We have the choice of letting Him produce this fruit in our lives.

Sometimes we might feel we have made so many mistakes it would be impossible for us to ever become a person of integrity. However, when we read the Bible we see God took some very unlikely people and wove them into the fabric of His family. Such a person was Rahab of Jericho. She lived a life of impurity, but she became a woman of faith (Hebrews 11:31), and is listed in the genealogy of Jesus (Matthew 1:5). Let's listen to her story.

REFLECTING HIS IMAGE
Rahab (Joshua 2:1–21; 6:17–25)

From outward appearance, I would have seemed the least likely person to be used by God. After all, I was a prostitute. But when spies arrived at my door one night, I was faced with a choice. I could turn them in or hide them. I chose to hide them, but only after making a deal.

You see, I knew what God had done for His people, the Israelites. How He dried up the water of the Red Sea when they came out of Egypt. How He utterly destroyed the two kings of the Amorites, Sihon and Og, on the other side of Jordan. I was terrified at the appearance of the Israelites on our borders. Would I commit treason? Help the enemy? Risk certain death? Absolutely! I knew I was lying, but my acts meant my family would survive an attack by Joshua and his army.

When the Israelites under Joshua's leadership crossed the Jordan River into Canaan, their access to the heart of the country was blocked by my city, Jericho. Joshua sent spies to look over the city. The plan was discovered, the city gates were closed, and the city guard set out on a house-to-house search to arrest the spies.

So, here they stood at my doorstep; two men, different from other men who came seeking my "favors." These were men of God, not idolaters. Instinctively, I knew I was willing to sacrifice my life for a cause I knew to be of God!

I led the two men up to the roof and hid them under the stalks of flax spread out there.

"Yes, two men did come to me," I told the soldiers later that night. "But I don't know where they are now. The men left at dark, when the gate was about to be shut. I don't know where they've gone. Hurry! Go after them. Maybe you can still catch them!" The soldiers hurried down the Jordan road toward the fords. As soon as they went by, the gate was shut. It was a perfect plan! My family's lives in exchange for the lives of two spies.

"Promise me," I pleaded to the spies, "that you will spare my father and mother, and everyone connected with my family." They agreed, and as I lowered them out a window with a rope, I told them, "Run for the hills and hide for three days. Then go on your way."

Before they ran, they also had instructions for me. I did as they said and hung a red rope outside my window. Gathering my entire family, we huddled close together inside my house. We were saved when the thunderous walls of Jericho collapsed around us!

And that's what happened. Amazing, isn't it? I'm thankful that God doesn't wait until people are perfect before He steps into their lives. First, God asked me to believe. Now—day by day—He is changing me.

I didn't have an impeccable reputation, but God accepted me anyway—maybe because I believed in God when it was dangerous to believe. Without any reservations, I switched my loyalty from the Canaanite gods to the true God of Israel. And that made all the difference. My family was saved from death, and I've been given a new home and a new people.

My choices, rather than my past, will define me for all time to come!

EMBRACING THE PENTECOSTAL PERSPECTIVE
What is the Holy Spirit teaching me?

Talk about a 180-degree turn! Rahab's testimony reads like a map detailing a hairpin curve. She moves from a life of desperation and degradation to one of hope, leadership, strength, and change. Her conversation with the spies demonstrates the tenacity needed to live a life of integrity. She held the spies to their promise, while simultaneously following through with her own obligations.

Has knowing Jesus made you a more tenacious person? If so, how?

Integrity calls for wholeness, without holes or weaknesses in the infrastructure. Have you ever stepped on—or rather, stepped through—a rotting log in the woods? Without the structural integrity of sound wood, the log cannot keep its shape, let alone support any weight. Lack of integrity always brings devastation, but tenacious integrity is the foundation for a life of meaning and power. The Holy Spirit infuses our previously flawed lives with healing wholeness, knitting our hearts with the heart of Jesus, and creating a life of integrity.

Share a positive encounter you have had with a person of integrity recently.

How has your integrity been tested this week?

Women are well-acquainted with the necessity of self-control. We cook elaborate holiday meals, complete with to-die-for desserts, and try not to gain a pound. We hit the grocery store with a rumbling stomach after a long day at work, and attempt to resist eating our way through every aisle. We search for bargains in the clothing department, only to face the "extravagantly-priced, oh-who-cares?-It's-Godiva" candy bar display at the department store cash register. Unfortunately, food temptations are not our greatest concern.

Since coming to Christ, how have you seen growth in your life in the area of self-control?

Where do you need the Spirit's help most in terms of self-control (e.g., eating, shopping, speaking kindly to your family, television–viewing habits)?

What practical helps have you learned that give you victory in times of temptation?

Do not confuse purity with naiveté. Purity is not incidental to the Christian life; it must be intentional. This means you cannot afford to take the ostrich (head in the sand) approach to your own or your family's purity. Studies now recognize one in six women (including

Christians) have an addiction to pornography. God's Word clearly and repeatedly teaches the difference between His plan for people, and the world's perversion of that plan.

Do you have an accountability partner? Do you hold one another accountable for issues of sexual purity (including the more subtle acts of inappropriate magazine reading or movie watching)?

What would you share with a young woman concerning God's guidance on issues of sexuality and purity?

How do you model purity for others around you?

INVITING GOD TO CHANGE MY VIEW
What change is God asking me to make?

The sport of gymnastics defies reason on several levels. A pint-sized athlete can demonstrate supersized power. Acts of incredible speed and momentum must be followed by "stuck" (unmoving) landings. A narrow beam provides the platform for a routine of skill and beauty. The illogical nature of these things fascinates, rather than repels, the average audience. The same could be said of the Christian life, for which gymnastics provides an apt analogy.

Believers are small in comparison to the strength needed for the activities and choices faced every day. They move at what seems to be an ever-increasing pace and yet are expected to remain "steadfast, immovable" in the Lord. Sometimes, the narrow way Jesus prescribes seems confining, when actually it gives the perfect platform for liberty and fulfillment of God-given purpose. The difference between human lack and God's perfection is made up by the power of the Spirit.

Will you confess a habit that is leading you away from purity? Would you like to experience more of the fruit of self-control? Do you need to give Christ first place in your life? Are your reading and television–viewing habits honoring the Lord? Do you lack the power to stick to your better intentions? Will you invite the Spirit to speak openly to you about your areas of weakness?

Prayer

Lord, thank You for calling me to a higher place of living through Jesus Christ. I have seen what the world offers, and I want nothing to do with it. Your way is better, and yet sometimes I am drawn in the opposite direction. Please fill me with Your Spirit so that I am only drawn to You and Your ways. Give me a heart so sensitive to pleasing You that I recoil instantly at temptation. Cleanse my thought life from entertaining anything that violates the purity of our relationship. I want to honor You with my inner life, outward appearance, and every word and action. I know this is only possible through Jesus. Amen.

JOURNALING

Take a few minutes to record your personal insights from the lesson.

HOW TO LEAD A
BIBLE STUDY GROUP

Welcome to the *Unlimited! . . . Bible Studies for Today's Pentecostal Woman* series! You will find these studies to be a great source for biblical guidance in living a Christian life in today's unsteady world, and for learning more about the Holy Spirit's work in your life.

Leading a group in studying these lessons will be challenging and rewarding, as together you discover how to apply God's Word to your life. You may have some questions about leading a Bible study. This section gives direction for answering the why, who, what, where, when, and how questions. Let's look at them individually.

"WHY" QUESTIONS
Why have a Bible study?

The first question you may ask is "Why do we want to have a Bible study?" This series is based on biblical, textual information, meant to be an expository study of what God's Word says on the topics presented in each lesson. Bill Bright, in his book *Discover the Book God Wrote,* says, "The Bible is so interconnected with God that we cannot separate it from His being. In fact, when we read the Bible with the right attitude, God, in the person of the Holy Spirit, joins with our spirit to help us understand it and apply it. The Book comes alive! The words in the Bible have life-changing power."[1]

Bible study group dynamics differ from other small group dynamics. Bible study is not necessarily easy, nor should those studying the

---

[1]Bill Bright, *Discover the Book God Wrote,* (Wheaton, Ill.: Tyndale House Publishers, Inc., 2003), 5.

Bible try to make it easy. Your main goal for beginning a Bible study should not be for a group to have fellowship, although fellowship will occur. If your main purpose is something other than a direct study of God's Word to gain biblical understanding for each member's life today, you may want to consider a different curriculum and format. The main goal of Bible study is to understand the Bible in a more profound way, so it will penetrate deeply into the hearts of those attending.

Bible study differs from traditional small groups in that fellowship can happen before and after the study, but not necessarily during. The Bible study sessions may become intense at times while group members grapple with the life issues presented in these lessons. Lives will be changed as a result of understanding God's Word.

If you combine Bible study with the small group dynamics of worship, prayer, and fellowship, then take that into consideration when planning the length of time for your sessions. Be sure the Bible study time is not crowded out by other activities.

"WHO" QUESTIONS
Who are the study members?

Who are you going to invite to this study? Many possibilities exist for establishing a Bible study group: neighbors (which is beneficial for evangelism), a new convert's study, a working woman's study, or an intergenerational study. Establishing the answer to this question helps answer some of the other questions.

Determine if you are going to establish a limit on the size of the group, and if you are going to allow newcomers to this study once it has started. A recommended size would be no less than four and no more than eleven members. A study group of twelve or more should be divided into smaller groups to facilitate discussion.

Who is the leadership?

Another "who" question is answered by determining who makes up the leadership of this study group. Will more than one person be a facilitator (teacher)? Will you need others in leadership? For example, do you want a group secretary to keep information such as names, addresses, and e-mail addresses of group members, in order to get information to each group member? Do you want a refreshment coordinator or special events coordinator if refreshments or fellowship events are to be a part of your time together? Who will these leaders be? These questions should be determined with the help of your church leadership. The women chosen for these positions need to be mature Christians.

"WHAT" QUESTIONS

The "what" questions will be partially answered when you answer the "who" questions. You may want to consider that these sessions would be valuable for a Sunday School class, or adapted as a couples' Bible study in addition to the suggested women's study groups. Don't limit these studies to just one audience.

Also ask "What will be our format for each session?" These Bible study lessons offer a format that is workable for your study group; however, each group should adapt the lesson components to fit its needs.

"WHERE" QUESTIONS

Where to hold the Bible study meetings may be determined when you know who is coming. Many settings can be used for these studies, including a room at the church, a restaurant's private room, the lunchroom of an office, a community center, or someone's home. Once a location is determined, for the strength of the meetings, do not change locations.

"WHEN" QUESTIONS

When will you meet for Bible study? What day will you meet? How long will the meeting last? How long will it take to complete this book?

These studies are planned so that each lesson can be taught in one session, for a total of eight sessions. However, if your group wants to meet for a shorter amount of time each week, the lessons could be taught in two parts, for a total of thirteen to sixteen sessions. **One and a half hours is a recommended time for each lesson** given in this series, assuming all lesson components are used in each session. Announce a planned start date and a final session date before beginning the unit of study.

The time of day for your meetings, of course, will be determined by the majority of the group attending, and the availability of the space you have chosen. You may want to build in time for fellowship before or after the Bible study; however, remember that it is better to have the study members wanting the meetings to be longer, rather than wishing they were shorter!

"HOW" QUESTIONS
How will you promote your Bible study sessions?

You may want to develop a brochure, place posters in the church hallways, ask for bulletin and pulpit announcements, or use any number of creative methods for getting information to potential group members. Be sure potential members understand how and where they can become involved in this study.

Carefully consider these questions and any others you may have to establish the framework for your Bible study. Trust God to be there as you meet together with other women to discover how to apply His Word to your life.

TIPS FOR BEING A BIBLE STUDY GROUP MEMBER

Each Bible study group member is important to the success of these Bible studies. Use these suggestions to help make your time together more meaningful.

- Agree to participate: The more fully each person participates, the more each group member benefits. Agree to study the lesson before the scheduled session, and agree to attend the sessions consistently to share the insight God gives you about each lesson. During discussions, contribute actively without straying from the discussion or dominating the group's time together.
- Respect each other: Through open and honest sharing we encourage one another. We can talk about who we are—our hurts, hopes, joys, and struggles—and what God is doing in us in this study. Each group member has valuable contributions to

make to these sessions, and comments of each member should be honored.

- Keep a confidence: What is shared by other study group members during study sessions should stay as part of the group and should not be talked about outside study session time.
- Affirm each other: Affirmation strengthens the body of Christ. We can recognize what is best in other members of this study group and encourage them to develop these qualities as we grow spiritually together.
- Pray: Write down the prayer requests of other study members and pray for these requests during the week. Be aware that other study members will be praying for you.

Allow the Holy Spirit to work in your life through these Bible studies. God bless your time together with Him!

TIPS FOR BEING A BIBLE STUDY LEADER

As a leader, you have a determining role in the effectiveness of your Bible study group. Many resources are available to help you. Here are a few tips for some of your responsibilities as a group leader:

Demonstrate personal commitment to Jesus, the Word, and the people you lead.

As a leader, your personal commitment to God is of utmost importance. Leading a group of believers demands a strong personal commitment to God and His Word. Are you growing spiritually as an individual believer? Do you enjoy interacting with people? Do you want to see others grow spiritually? Then you will most likely be able to successfully lead a Bible study group.

Prepare thoroughly in prayer, study, and with a heart for the members of your group.

Use extra study helps if needed, such as Bible concordances, dictionaries, and study Bibles. Write notes in the margin of this study guide to help you facilitate discussion.

Decide before the first session if you will use every component offered in these lessons, or if you will choose only some of the components. See "Understanding and Using the Lesson Components" below for more information concerning each lesson segment.

The format for teaching these lessons will be interactive lecture, and group reflection and discussion. Be so familiar with the lesson content beforehand that you will be able to keep the group moving forward in the lesson. Ask each study member to read the lesson and write out answers before coming to the session so they will also be ready for discussion.

Facilitate discussion. Know your group and the lesson well enough to carefully select key questions that will generate interaction; resist the temptation to lecture.

Keep the conversations biblically grounded by sticking to the topic of each lesson. Move on to the next question, rather than allowing silence or "down" time, unless the silence is meaningful to the question being considered.

Guard a nurturing environment; encourage uplifting conversation, do not permit gossip, and insist on confidentiality. As possible, involve all study group members in the discussion at some time.

Always invite God's presence in your study sessions. Open and close each session with prayer, not as a formality, but a heartfelt necessity.

UNDERSTANDING AND USING THE LESSON COMPONENTS

You will find consistency in the components of each lesson of this book. An explanation of each component is given to clarify the purpose of each segment, enriching your total study experience.

CATCHING SIGHT
Introduction

The first component, "Catching Sight," directs the reader and study group to the topic of the lesson. Usually an anecdote or true-life story begins each lesson, followed by a brief explanation of the topic. Use these introductions to capture the attention of your group members as they are getting settled. If you are using this series for independent study, this introduction should help focus your mind as you begin.

GETTING FOCUSED
Begin your study by sharing thoughts on the following:

This component of the lesson initiates group discussion on the lesson topic. Break into groups of three to five to discuss the question or statement given in "Getting Focused." If you are studying independently, write down your thoughts on the question or statement. If you are leading a group, ask the group members to look at this question before the session and jot down some thoughts to facilitate discussion.

BIBLE READING

Bible passages selected to accompany each lesson are given in two versions: the New International Version and the *New Living Translation*. These two versions are side by side for easy reference during lesson study.

Shorter Bible readings may be read aloud by an individual or by the group. Longer readings should be read by group members before the session. Portions of the longer reading can be read during study time.

GAINING BIBLICAL INSIGHT

This component is the biblical exposition of the lesson. The pivotal truth of the lesson is given in italics beneath the component section heading. This is the "truth in a nutshell" concerning the topic of the lesson.

REFLECTING HIS IMAGE

This component gives an opportunity for creativity, as well as portraying the truth of the lesson. The Bible woman reflects the incarnation of the lesson's truths, and in most cases is given as an example of a life to emulate. This component can be used in several ways:

Individual devotional reading: Ask each group member to read this portion before coming to the study.

Small-group reading: Assign one person to read this component at the appropriate time in class or ask several to women read parts.

Drama: Assign women to portray each character in the Bible story and a narrator. Ask the women to give their practiced dramatic portrayal at an appropriate time in the study. Simple costumes will complete the effect.

Monologue: Request that one woman practice portraying the Bible woman in the lesson, and present a dramatic monologue during the study.

EMBRACING THE PENTECOSTAL PERSPECTIVE
What is the Holy Spirit teaching me?

This perspective of a Pentecostal believer begins by asking, "What is the Holy Spirit teaching me?" We believe the Holy Spirit is a unique Person of the Trinity with a specific ministry in the life of a Christian. The questions raised in this component will help the Pentecostal believer to apply the truths of the lesson in her own life.

INVITING GOD TO CHANGE MY VIEW
What change is God asking me to make?

After interacting with God's Word, seeing it in another woman's life, and discerning how it applies to one's own, there is one more essential step before we can live differently in light of the truth— prayer! This section provides questions that help each participant to go to the heart of the issue, asking God to bring change where it is most needed. Notice that there is usually a question provided to open the door for someone to receive Christ as Savior. A prayer is also included as a sample, a starting point, or simply as personal reflection.

JOURNALING
Take a few moments to record your personal insights from the lesson.

Space is given at the end of each lesson for writing down personal thoughts and reflections that transpire during the study of each lesson. The Bible study leader can take time for this in class or request that members complete this on their own time after the session.

ARLENE ALLEN
—Catching Sight

The teacup collection that she keeps is a testament to the Southern hospitality one receives when meeting Arlene Allen. Born in the Appalachian mountains of Virginia, she never fails to delight and challenge her audiences with her quick wit and Southern-style wisdom.

An ordained minister with the Assemblies of God, Arlene is the director for the national Women's Ministries Department. She serves on the boards of the national Women in Ministry Task Force, Religious Alliance Against Pornography, and Global Pastors' Wives Network. She has an extensive speaking history that includes pulpit ministry, leadership training, and women's and ministers' wives retreats.

Arlene has been married for thirty-nine years to Gary R. Allen who serves as the executive coordinator of the Ministerial Enrichment office of the Assemblies of God. The Allens are parents of two sons and the proud grandparents of two "incredible" grandsons, Grant and Jacob.

PEGGY MUSGROVE
—Gaining Biblical Insight

In her book, *Musings of a Maraschino Cherry,* Peggy Musgrove talks about the role of a pastor's wife as sometimes like being the cherry on top of an ice cream sundae. But her life and ministry has been far more than just mere decoration.

Peggy is a speaker and freelance writer. Previously, she served as national director of Women's Ministries for the Assemblies of God and director of Women's Ministries for the Kansas District Assemblies of God. Peggy's written works include *Who's Who Among Bible Women,*

Pleasing God, Praying Always, and articles for several publications. Peggy holds two bachelor of arts degrees, one from Wichita State University and one from Central Bible College.

Peggy and her husband Derald served local churches and in district ministy in Kansas before moving in 1993 to Springfield, Missouri, where they both served in national offices for the Assemblies of God. They have two daughters, two "utterly awesome grandsons" and one "fabulously wonderful granddaughter."

When she's not writing, Peggy enjoys many things—reading, playing games, family holidays and vacations, spending time with her grandkids and friends, traveling with her husband, and antique shopping.

LORI O'DEA
—Embracing the Pentecostal Perspective & Inviting God to Change My View

With discipleship being the passion of her ministry, Lori serves as the doctor of ministry coordinator and visiting professor of practical theology for the Assemblies of God Theological Seminary (AGTS). Previously, Lori served on pastoral staffs in churches in Decatur, Illinois, and Waterford, Michigan.

Lori was born and raised in Michigan and spent eight years in Illinois before relocating to her current home in Springfield, Missouri. She shares her home with her awesome cat, named Zipper, whom she claims can sail through the air like Michael Jordan. Aviation is one of her many interests and someday she would like to get her pilot's license. She's a firm believer that Mountain Dew, Doritos, and chocolate will be served in vast quantities at the Marriage Supper of the Lamb, though she has yet to find biblical support for her hopes.

Lori has spent a lot of time hitting the books and her educational credentials prove it. She earned a bachelor of science in missions and evangelism from Southwestern Assemblies of God University, her master of divinity with a dual emphasis in biblical languages and pastoral ministry, and a doctor of ministry in Pentecostal leadership from AGTS. In addition, Lori has served as a contributor to the *Complete Biblical Library* and *Enrichment Journal*.

CANDY TOLBERT
—Reflecting His Image

She may have been transplanted to Missouri, but Candy Tolbert is a California girl at heart. She is a woman who "thinks out loud" about her love of God, love of spouse, love of children, and her passion for seeing other women reach their full potential in Christ. A licensed minister with the Assemblies of God for twenty-five years, Candy is the national leadership development coordinator for Women's Ministries.

Her extensive background includes public speaking, Christian education, missions, university student ministry, children's ministry, and music ministry. She has written articles appearing in the *Sunday School Counselor*, *Spirit Led Woman* and *Woman's Touch* magazines.

Candy is married to the love of her life, Michael, to whom she has been married for twenty-five years. Together they pastored several churches in the Southern California area. Candy is also the proud mom of two daughters, Rachel and Ashley. Candy's other passions in life include home decorating and good coffee.